A different kind of power

A different kind of power
Miles Olsen

Copyright © Miles Olsen 2024

All rights reserved.

No part of this book may be reproduced or used in any manner without written permission of the copyright owner except for the use of quotations in a book review.

The events and conversations in this book have been set down to the best of the author's ability, although names and details have been changed to protect the privacy of individuals.

First paperback edition September 2024
ISBN 978-1-7774652-6-1 (paperback)

milesolsen.com

One

After three years alone, it was time to make a change. I had grown so used to the peace and calm of being by myself that the prospect of meeting new people, dating, and searching for a partner had become somewhat terrifying. But I knew that I needed to step out of my shell. My solitude had become comfortable and familiar - too comfortable and familiar. And so I prepared myself to shatter it one step at a time.

Before I could begin my search for love, however, the first order of business was to get my apartment ready. If I was ever going to bring a woman there without embarrassing myself, my humble residence needed some serious revitalization. Maybe because I hadn't considered inviting a romantic interest there in years, I'd neglected turning my tiny studio apartment from a house into a home. I had been living in that place for half a decade - yet I existed there like a vagrant, never fully taking root, embracing where I was, and turning the space into something that felt like my own.

A different kind of power

The apartment had come furnished when I moved in - complete with a futon, basic kitchen equipment, and, among other things, a cheap, plastic, swivelling office chair that sat in a corner of the small living space. A year earlier, I had been lounging in that plastic chair when its backrest suddenly broke off from the pressure of my body leaning against it, sending me crashing onto the floor. In the shock of that moment, I felt a wave of anger at the chair as though it had betrayed my trust. But instead of immediately throwing the defective piece of furniture away, I kept it. The broken backrest remained barely attached to its swivelling seat, drooping toward the ground - but otherwise, it was still a perfectly functional chair.

Months later, when my friend Pandora visited, she looked at that pitiful broken seat in confusion and said: "Miles, you can afford a new chair. Why do you still have that thing?"

"It works," I replied. "And I'm a minimalist - I don't care about material things."

She shook her head in disbelief and muttered: "Clearly."

What seemed absurd and dilapidated to my friend was something I had accepted and learned to live with quite happily. But now, as I surveyed my curious little home, I knew that broken plastic chair was the first thing that needed to go, and I took it downstairs to the garbage. Along with it went the tacky futon cover I'd never liked and an assortment of mismatched, worn-out items I'd obtained for free (or near-free) over the years

One

that had served their purpose and could now be given away or disposed of.

Over two weeks, I made numerous trips to various stores, first buying a nice new chair, then a matching rug to lie beneath it and a variety of other simple items to bring life, order, and dignity to my humble home. It didn't take long before I began to feel quite happy about how my living space looked.

While my plan to start dating (and to have a bit of self-respect as I approached that endeavour) had been the catalyst for this makeover, bringing such simple changes to my environment was something that, on its own, improved my quality of life. I was no longer surrounded by a cluttered, thoughtless assortment of stuff that I didn't like and was too lazy or complacent to do anything about. There was now some degree of care and intention around me, even if the superficial changes to my residence had been minor.

While finishing this home makeover, I downloaded a few of the most popular dating apps onto my phone. I made profiles for myself on them that I hoped would accurately depict who I was at that moment: A guy in his thirties who hadn't dated or been in a relationship for years, who worked evenings in a restaurant as a waiter, and who, by day, was an indie author pursuing his creative dreams.

The last time I felt this ready to go out and find love, the world came crashing to a halt because of a global pandemic. But this time was going to be different. I was more stable now. I'd learned so much. My apartment actually looked nice. I was getting excited to meet new

A different kind of power

people and go on some dates. And then, I got a phone call.

I was preparing to head out for a late shift at the restaurant when my Dad called out of the blue. He rarely phoned spontaneously, so I was surprised as I answered: "Hey Dad, how's it going?"

My Father sighed and said: "Oh, I've had better days."

With a quiet exasperation in his voice, he proceeded to share that he'd just been diagnosed with an aggressive form of skin cancer and would begin treatment immediately.

"They say it's good that we caught it early on," he told me, "and that if they can remove all the cancer now, so long as it hasn't spread, I'll be fine."

As we spoke for the following ten minutes, I slowly began to understand the gravity of what my Dad was telling me. I felt a painful lump develop in the back of my throat as I strained to hold back tears.

"I'll be going in for surgery next week," he continued, "so that's good. And I can only be positive. Complaining and getting negative about this isn't going to help. So I've just gotta make the best of it. I've gotta look at the bright side. You know, the nurses at the hospital were all so nice - really good people. And I got them laughing pretty good, too. We were all laughing so hard!"

He paused for a moment before adding: "Everyone so far has been great. And that's all I can ask for."

As I listened to my Father, I was moved by his positivity and stoic acceptance of the reality at hand -

One

though I heard something deeper in his voice that let me know how serious this situation might be. We spoke for a while longer, and then I told him that I loved him, and we said goodbye as I headed out the door on my way to work.

Over the following days, the weight of my Dad's news sank in. My parents were getting older, and though I always knew this meant that one day - a day far from now - they might be gone, this was the first time the harsh truth of their mortality had brushed past me. Nobody's life was imminently ending, and no tragedy was immediately at hand - but mortality had entered into the conversation, and it shook me.

I reflected on how much my Father meant to me and how I wasn't ready for him to leave. It wasn't time yet. There were more conversations I needed to have with him, more love and laughter to share. As I digested his situation, I felt a strange mix of emotions.

Then, I got an idea: I would write a book. For some time, I had known that one day, I planned on writing a book that honoured my Dad and his presence in my life. I figured it would be a project I got around to in several years. But I knew for sure that I wanted to write something to shine a light on my Father and what he meant to me. The book I envisioned wouldn't be directly about him - his presence would be woven into a bigger story throughout its pages. And in my gut, I knew I had to do this eventually - it would be a kind of love letter to my parents that I could share with the world.

A different kind of power

At this point in time, however, it had been just two years since I published my most recent book. I fully expected to wait until that book had blown up and become an international bestselling sensation before I stepped back into the painful, arduous process of writing another one. I even had an exact number of copies I promised myself I needed to sell before I would consider starting another project: Ten thousand books. So far, it had been two years, and I had sold about two hundred copies. In other words, it didn't look like that next book would happen anytime soon.

But suddenly, given the moment's urgency, that distant goal was irrelevant. Selling a specific number of copies seemed pointless and superficial. I didn't know how long my Dad would be around, so the potential book I planned on writing at some point in the distant future needed to be written now. In fact, it needed to be done as soon as possible. So I got to work.

For the next seven months, I focused on completing this task. Not long after beginning writing, I deleted all the dating apps I had recently downloaded. I had yet to exchange messages with a single woman on them, but that didn't matter anymore - something much more urgent required my attention.

It didn't take long to remember why I'd wanted to avoid writing another book again so soon: I couldn't stop once I started. It was like I struck a vein that produced a steady flow of creative energy. And once that flow was established, I worried that if I was inactive and let it sit idle for too long, it would disappear. So, I coddled and protected that current of

One

words and ideas. If I missed my writing sessions for several days in a row, I was filled with a horrible sense of anxiety that I might have lost something precious. But whenever I came back to it, the words flowed. And eventually, I stopped getting distracted.

Aside from writing, my life was incredibly simple during this time. I worked evenings at the restaurant, where I had the great fortune of interacting with a river of humanity and could fill my cup with social connection. In the mornings, I walked in the forest religiously for an hour or more, clearing my mind, giving my nervous system a much-needed break from technological overstimulation, and mapping out the next steps in my creative process. And then, I wrote.

I spent less time with friends than usual, but that was okay. Something beautiful filled my world, and I was determined to see it through to completion.

The longer I worked on that book, the more I felt like it was healing something in me - like the creative act was a way of finding my power, locating a deeper strength in my voice, and shedding an old, dead layer of skin. When I paused occasionally and reflected on the mission I'd been focused on right before I got that call from my Father (to meet women and date), I wondered if, somehow, this work was anchoring me into a strength that I needed to have a grip on before embarking on that journey.

A different kind of power

I was putting the finishing touches on this project when I got word that, to the enormous relief of my entire family, my Father had successfully completed his cancer treatment and was given a clean bill of health. We were all grateful beyond words and touched by how he handled the stress and uncertainty of this ordeal. The grind of appointments, biopsies, surgery, and countless hours spent in the soul-crushing waiting rooms and hallways of hospitals was, by its very nature, demoralizing. But my Father had kept his sense of humour and levity throughout it.

And, as scary as this brush with fate had been, it had pushed me to communicate my love for my Dad to him clearly - to hold nothing back. In fact, it pushed me so hard that I now had a finished book, which was sparked by this sobering event. And, after months of work, it was ready to be shared with him and the world.

When I published this book of stories and announced it to my small network of friends, acquaintances, and readers near the end of spring, I felt excited. This was the most honest and raw thing I'd ever written, and I really believed in it. And after working for a few years at building an audience, I was hopeful this book would be more superficially successful than anything I'd done previously. I looked at the sales of my last book and wondered how many of those readers would

One

immediately buy a copy of my new one. Probably quite a few of them, I thought.

So, with reasonably high hopes and a feeling of love for this new creation in my heart, I shared it with my tiny corner of the world and waited for the magic to start. While money was not my inspiration to write this book, I realized that it would be nice to make some cash from all the sales that were about to pour in.

In the days after launching it, I checked my sales dashboard somewhat compulsively - too curious to resist the temptation to see what was happening in real-time. And then, I saw the first official sale.

"Amazing," I thought to myself.

The next time I checked, there were two more sales.

"It has begun," I gleefully observed.

When I checked the following day, there were four more sales. By that evening, close to ten units had been ordered. And then, it all stopped.

Days passed, and to my utter astonishment and disbelief, no more books were sold. A week went by, and the numbers stayed the same. Then another week came and went - no sales. As time marched on and no more books were sold, I felt like something was wrong with reality. This seemed like a bad dream.

A month passed, and little changed. The wave of book sales I'd been anticipating never arrived. This was so far from my humblest expectations that I almost had to pinch myself to make sure that I was awake. But I was fully conscious, and this was real life - it was just unfolding in a shape that was nothing like what I'd imagined. As my hopes and expectations shattered, I was deflated by a profoundly underwhelming response to this labour of love I had shared with the world.

Even my closest friends seemed preoccupied with their own lives and worries at that moment and showed little or no interest in reading this book of mine. So, instead of the thunderous applause and life-changing success I'd been expecting, I tasted the bitter tonic of silence and obscurity. And while my ego was writhing in embarrassment at the humbling reality of the moment, I was aware that this was all probably good for my heart.

One of the few people who did read that book right away was my Dad - the man who had inspired its creation in the first place. When I spoke to him immediately after he finished it, his words were simple and straightforward.

"Well, I'm not much of a reader," he said, "so it took me a few days, but I just finished."

"What did you think?" I asked, with a vulnerability that is probably only possible between a child and their Father.

"Oh, it was good," he replied. "I liked it. Yep, your Mother and I, we really liked it."

He paused for a moment before adding: "You sure do pour your soul onto the page."

Beneath those words was something that felt like a mix of respect and shock at what his son had made. We

One

talked briefly about the stories in the book, my Dad's health, and life in general before saying goodbye.

I left that conversation with a warm, glowing sensation in my chest - and the satisfying knowledge that this book's primary mission had been fulfilled: The person who inspired it had received it - and I got the impression that his heart had received it, too.

For the next few weeks, as I came to terms with the superficially disappointing performance of my book launch, I noticed a spark in me that felt shockingly bright, alive, and well. I had shared something that came from my heart, that was meant to be a kind of love note to my parents - which they had received and accepted. So, as lacklustre as the reality of my life as an author appeared on the surface, something indescribably powerful was happening inside of me. I knew in my gut that it was all perfect - that my lack of external success was good medicine and had nothing to do with another kind of success that lived at a deeper level.

It's probably worth mentioning that during this time, I began to receive a slow trickle of messages from strangers about the book. These were people, sometimes from across the world, who were writing to say how much that little book of stories meant to them. And, each time I received one of these notes, I was hit with the reality that no matter how small the number of people this work was reaching, if it touched one heart, that alone was immeasurably significant.

A different kind of power

By now, it had been over half a year since I first declared that it was time to push myself out of my solitary shell - and I had not begun my mission of dating or pursuing a partnership in any meaningful way. But, as I found myself straying down a different path, I sensed there was some kind of perfection to this change in priorities. It was almost as though the moment I announced to life that I was ready to find love, it had answered: *Oh, you're ready to love? We have the perfect thing for you - the perfect place to put that love! But it doesn't look anything like what you've imagined...*

I had failed entirely to begin dating, but I reconciled myself with the knowledge that I had found another place to share love. And I assured myself that, someday soon, I'd be out there, meeting new people.

Two

While I was in the midst of launching my new book, I received a message from an old hometown acquaintance that piqued my curiosity. She was writing to tell me that my high school reunion was happening later that spring, and I was invited. To my surprise, I instantly felt I needed to go to this reunion with a sense of urgency so strong it was confusing.

It was completely out of character for me to light up at the chance to revisit this chapter of my past. I had not enjoyed high school, dropping out during my twelfth-grade year in frustration. The entire experience had been a lonely and miserable phase of life. And when it was over, I was happy to move on, with no intention of ever looking back.

But as I read this invitation and imagined walking into a room filled with all the souls I was uncomfortable and self-conscious around as a teen, it felt like an opportunity I couldn't pass up. A deep part of me desperately wanted to go.

A different kind of power

But rather than acting from my gut and responding to this invite immediately, I postponed making a final decision. There was something vulnerable about making a choice so out of character - travelling a significant distance to my hometown for a reunion with a group of people who might not remember me (and if they did, might wonder why on earth I had come there).

When I spoke to my parents about this reunion, my Mom assumed I wouldn't go: "That doesn't sound like something you would enjoy," she said.

"I know," I replied. "It's kind of crazy, but a part of me feels like I have to go. Maybe something healing could come out of it. I always felt like an alien in high school. And going back to that awkward social situation now, as an adult - it might be really revealing."

I explained that I was curious what all the kids I grew up with were like now. How had these years of life softened or hardened them? Who had they become? I crossed paths with each of them at such a tender and fertile crossroads - so many things would have changed for each of us since then. It seemed far too fascinating an opportunity to ignore.

But part of me still wanted to avoid the vulnerability of registering for the event, and I hesitated. It wasn't until the final day before registration closed that I pushed past my resistance and sent the small fee to sign up for it. Once that was settled and done, I began to brace myself for what might be a seismically weird and awkward experience. I booked a week off from work around the date of the reunion, somewhat in shock that I was going to do this - and that, for some strange

Two

reason, it felt like a matter of utmost significance to my heart. It felt like the most important thing I needed to do.

As the event's date approached in mid-June, I reserved a rental car for the trip to my hometown. I planned on staying with my parents and spending quality time with them, attending the reunion, and trekking around the area.

My initial vision for this trip was triumphant: Having recently finished my new book, this would be a chance to cut loose and enjoy life, soak in the beauty of nature, and have an all-around celebratory, revitalizing experience. I'd wanted to arrange a book signing event in my hometown that coincided with the reunion. But when I contacted local bookstores, I heard nothing back from them.

This didn't bother me. I thought it might even be better to enjoy the experience of visiting family and attending the reunion without distractions.

The morning I left the city and travelled homeward, I started to come down with a cold. To my dismay, this illness only got worse over the following days. So, instead of revelling in the beauty of the countryside, I found myself sick and tired, with little energy for anything. It was great to see my parents and catch up in person. But, after the first day, I was directionless and deflated - drained from the sickness that had taken hold of my body.

As I spent the next few days dragging myself out of my parents' home on little expeditions to old stomping grounds, I felt a sense of desolation. Perhaps as a way of bracing for the painful comparisons that were about to confront me at my high school reunion, I walked down the streets and forest paths I'd frequented in my youth and reflected on the life I'd gone on to live with shame and regret. During my earlier years, I'd gleefully flouted any sense of convention or normalcy, embracing a path guided by my heart rather than a desire for social acceptance or material stability. Now, I was living in the wake of those choices: A grown man with no conventional career (a waiter in a restaurant and the author of a new book that had sold almost a dozen copies) - no wife, kids, mortgage, degree, etc. Normally, I could see the beauty in all this, but not now. There was something about the elements of that moment - the illness (which made me less emotionally resilient than usual), the humbling juncture I was at in my life as a writer, and the spectre of going to this reunion - that together created a perfect storm and brought me to a place of despondency and discomfort in my own skin that I hadn't felt since… high school.

My cold had mostly passed by the afternoon of the reunion, so I couldn't use it as an excuse not to go. In the days leading up to the event, I'd reached out to a few old friends and acquaintances I hoped would be there - specific individuals I knew I would be comfortable enough with to latch onto and use as a kind of social

Two

shield. Unfortunately, none of them were nearby or had any desire to go.

So, I realized I would be entering this situation with no shield - no familiar old pal to stand beside or cling to as I faced the onslaught of awkwardness. I was going to have to walk into this storm alone.

In the hours before the event, I paced around my parents' backyard and wondered if it would be okay to just call this off. "I don't really need to put myself through this, do I? Nobody knows I'm going - why bother with it?" I came up with numerous reasons to cancel my mission as the reality I was heading into began to feel like a monster breathing down my neck.

But, I reasoned with myself, I had travelled all this way. And no matter how horrible or embarrassing my experience was, I knew it would be interesting. I also knew I wouldn't regret going and making a fool of myself - but I would regret it forever if I let my fear stop me. So, I got ready to leave. I put on the freshly pressed black dress shirt I'd brought for the occasion, got into my rental car, and started to drive.

I took a long route to the hall where the event was being held. Because I had no one there who was expecting me - or who I knew I would be comfortable sitting down and talking with when I arrived - showing up late and blending into a busy crowd seemed ideal.

As I slowly drove to my destination, the level of insecurity and panic that my body was overcome by shocked me. I was so nervous that I began to sweat profusely in the air-conditioned rental car - my armpits stinging from this adrenalized perspiration.

A different kind of power

I took some deep breaths to calm down and get centred, pulling over on a quiet backroad to remind myself that this was not actually a scary thing - I was just going to say hello to a bunch of strangers I used to go to high school with. Then, I noticed an acrid smell - my body was so nervous that it was producing a powerful, rank odour. My stinging, sweaty armpits were emanating this disturbingly potent stench. Confused and horrified, I couldn't remember my body making a smell anything like this since... high school.

As I sat in the little rental car, I realized what was happening: I was regressing - first emotionally and now physiologically - to my teenage state. It was extraordinary. I smelled like a nervous sixteen-year-old with no deodorant (despite having put my regular deodorant on just before leaving). And the sour stench I was now emitting made me feel even more self-conscious, feeding the nervousness that was causing it. Thankfully, I noticed that as long as I kept my arms down and against my side, my armpits were sealed shut, and the smell was more or less contained. With a mixture of embarrassment and wonder, I continued on to my destination.

After parking a few blocks away from the hall my classmates had rented for this reunion, I walked to my destination along a quiet, small-town street on the warm June evening. I kept my armpits closed tight and readied myself for whatever awaited. As I approached the venue, I saw a man about my age smoking a cigarette near the entrance - I said hello but had no idea who he was.

Two

Then, as I stepped through the front door of the building, I found a large banquet hall filled with dozens of people talking in little groups, most of whom had alcoholic beverages in hand. Sitting near the entrance at a small table was the lead organizer of the event, Lina - a woman I'd known and remembered from high school.

We exchanged a warm, slightly awkward hello before I wandered alone toward the crowd and wondered what the hell I'd gotten myself into. I recognized nearly every face in that room, but nobody stood out as an obvious person to gravitate toward. Almost everyone was engaged in some kind of friendly conversation, and I stood dumbfounded at the edge of it all. Then, I did the only obvious thing: I headed straight to the bathroom.

Nobody was in there, but just to ensure a moment of privacy, I walked into an empty stall and closed the door. Having seen the reality of the mess I'd gotten myself into, I needed to get my head together and figure out a plan.

"Okay," I thought, "I know you want to disappear, but you can't. This is painful in the very best way possible. Right now, you're going to have to face the awkwardness you ran from as a kid. You're going to have to march up to these people you hid from in the past and shamelessly start talking to them. Be kind, be open, and talk to every person in that room - there's no turning back now."

I took a few deep breaths before leaving that stall's privacy, washing my hands, and stepping back into the crowded hall. As self-conscious as I was to be there alone, I was also sincerely excited to see almost everyone in that room. The first person I said hello to was Allan Ford, who I remembered sitting in front of in grade seven. We'd never been friends but shared the same classrooms, school buses, and hallways for years.

"Allan Ford? It's amazing to see you!" I exclaimed with unrestrained affection.

"What the hell - Miles Olsen?" Allan said, clearly surprised by my presence. "Holy crap, man. Good to see you!"

We exchanged a firm handshake, and before I could trip over myself trying to start a conversation, he turned around and continued talking to someone he'd previously been chatting with. I recognized who he was speaking to - Eric Willis - and offered another warm greeting to Eric. He smiled and shook my hand, and when the two of them immediately resumed their conversation, I got the hint that this wasn't the place for me to stick around and talk, so I awkwardly moved along.

There was something perfectly weird about that whole interaction - I felt undeterred and was excited to have broken the ice and gotten this party started. As I scanned my surroundings for the next familiar face to approach, I noticed a woman smiling at me from the corner of the room. As we made eye contact, she exclaimed: "Miles!" and stood up to greet me. It was Karol Kolbourn, one of my old pals from art class with whom I'd always had a lot of fun and laughs. I hadn't even thought about how great it would be to see Karol there - but the moment I heard her voice, I realized that I

Two

had officially found my "shield" person - that one individual who I knew liked me and who I could go stand beside or talk to without feeling like a burden. She was sitting with Ray Nichols, another of the art-class kids I used to have so much fun goofing around with, and I greeted them both with a huge grin.

"I can't believe you're here, Miles," Karol beamed. "I'm so happy to see you!"

I shared Karol's excitement, and the three of us immediately started joking about how painful this whole spectacle was and how we'd all resisted signing up for it until the very last minute. We acknowledged that, for each of us, the opportunity to see how everyone had grown and changed was simply too fascinating to pass up.

Then, before my old pals could notice the sour odour that I was emanating and wonder what was wrong with me, I openly acknowledged it: "You want to know something crazy?" I asked. Karol and Ray nodded with curiosity, and I continued: "On the drive here, I felt so anxious and afraid that I started producing the body odour of my sixteen-year-old self. Seriously, I just showered and I'm wearing deodorant, but it didn't stand a chance against this. I think that coming back to this social situation produced a very specific kind of fear in me - one that my body hasn't felt since high school. And it's making me emit this crazy, awful smell that I can only remember from being a teenager. It's fascinating and incredibly embarrassing."

A different kind of power

Karol's jaw dropped as she stared at me in disbelief: "What the hell, Miles," she said. "The exact same thing happened to me on my way here!"

Karol explained that as she drove to the reunion, she'd also begun to feel so anxious that she started sweating and stinking like a sixteen-year-old with bad hygiene. But unlike me, she had stopped at a convenience store and bought some deodorant, which saved her from the embarrassment I was about to endure.

"The deodorant's in my car if you want to use it," she graciously added.

Realizing Karol was serious about this offer, I didn't hesitate before taking her up on it. It felt like a kind of divine intervention. So, laughing about our strange shared crises, we stepped out of the crowded hall and walked toward her vehicle. When we arrived at her car, she retrieved a freshly opened stick of Old Spice *Night Panther* deodorant. As she handed it to me, we joked about how this Night Panther was saving both of our nights and lost ourselves laughing uncontrollably like we had so many years earlier.

As we made our way back into the commotion, I learned that Karol had been happily married for many years and was a mother to several children - the oldest of whom was now almost a teenager. She lived a simple, beautiful life in the countryside. Ray was also married with children, and it made me happy to see how much joy he had in his voice as he spoke about his life as a husband and father. It was a relief to discover how easy, fun, and natural it was talking with these two sweet

Two

souls. But now that I had gotten the ball rolling, I had to force myself back into the crowd to interact with my other former classmates.

After surveying the different people I could start with, I approached a group of women - all of whom I recognized and would have considered the popular girls back in high school. I recalled having slight crushes on a couple of them back in the day. But tonight, I wasn't interested in any funny business. I was there to be sincerely present to this experience, not to indulge in any long-forgotten romantic feelings or fixations that could easily distract me or absorb my attention.

As I approached this group, I realized that I knew exactly who each of these women was, and they almost certainly would recognize me from our school years together - but I had probably never spoken directly to any of them. Then, I made my move, choosing to put my most awkward foot forward as I walked up to them and said: "Hi, I'm Miles, and I don't think I ever really talked to any of you during high school because I was a very shy and insecure kid - but I recognize all of you, and you all seemed really cool back then. It's awesome to see you here."

The group of women looked at me and let out a unanimous "Awww," seemingly appreciative of my candour. They recognized me as clearly as I recognized them, and we spoke for the next few minutes. I learned that some of them had husbands and several children, and some were divorced with children. It seemed that I was one of the only people under that roof who hadn't made any babies yet.

Before arriving that evening, I had prepared a simple description of my life, knowing that I would be bombarded countless times with the question, "What do you do?"

I'd always struggled with that question and choked up when confronted by it. But once I gave my response some thought, a simple and honest answer revealed itself: *I live in Vancouver, where I work evenings as a waiter in a restaurant, write books, and walk around in nature.*

As expected, this question came up with almost everyone I spoke to. When I was chatting with the popular girls, I was surprised by their common reaction when I told them what I was doing with my life - they thought it sounded great.

When I shared my life update with Natalie Barker (who had sat beside me in grade ten English class and I remembered having a crush on), her response was: "That's amazing, Miles! You're chasing your dreams - that's so cool. I wish I was that brave. You'll never regret going for it." She spoke with conviction, and a few others around us nodded and smiled in agreement. I explained the drawbacks and self-consciousness I felt having chosen an unconventional and uncertain life path. But as I spoke, Natalie didn't seem to believe my words.

"I don't know, Miles. It sounds like you're living the dream - a simple, quiet life close to nature while in the city, creating your art and in love with your surroundings. As a busy mom and a burned-out schoolteacher, I'm jealous."

Two

We went on to speak about various things, from trauma and healing to our strange grade ten English teacher, Mr. Ladner. When the conversation faded, I turned around and started talking to another familiar face. I asked this classmate about his life, and he asked about mine. Then, I drifted to another conversation. Then another. Once I got the wheels turning, I realized this wasn't so bad. My years of walking up to strangers as a waiter - constantly interrupting groups of people and interjecting my presence into their social bubble - had prepared me for this.

Making my way around the crowd, I was shocked by how open-minded, supportive, and sincere everyone seemed to be. Maybe it was that we were all excited to see each other and were connected to one another's youth and innocence in a very particular way. We were all many years removed from our time together, but my heart remembered all of these people as fresh-faced, vibrant, and optimistic kids who could be anyone they wanted to be and do anything they wanted to do in the whole wide world. Whatever limitations, heartbreaks or failures they may have endured since then, they still lived in my imagination as pure, limitless youth.

One of the most interesting conversations of the night happened when I crossed paths with Marcus Fitzgerald. As a kid, I had wandered through the same hallways as Marcus for many years, yet I don't think we ever truly spoke. After I chatted with his wife for a few minutes, she insisted that he and I talk immediately. She disappeared into the crowd to find him, and a few minutes later, Marcus approached me with a big, bright, toothy smile. He gave me a strong handshake before I asked him how his life had been so far.

Marcus shared a synopsis of his experiences: He had indulged in some early years of partying and hedonism, followed by a spiral into addiction, and then a complete change of direction through embracing sobriety. By now, he had been sober for many years. He appeared to have approached his recovery with the same intensity that he might have previously directed to partying. Marcus described his exploration of a variety of healing methods and wellness practices, from ayahuasca ceremonies and the use of other psychedelics to more straightforward spiritual and emotional work. He acknowledged how psychedelics and spirituality could be their own trap - and how, given the extreme nature of his personality, things that seemed healthy on the surface (such as self-improvement or mindfulness practices) could be dangerous.

"I'm so intense with things," he said, "that I'll start meditating for a week and then get so excited that I want to sell everything I own, move to India, and become a monk. It's a blessing and a curse to be such an extreme person. I guess it's something in me that I'm just learning to watch."

I listened to Marcus with awe. In him, I saw a brother on a very similar path - someone who'd been playing with spirituality for long enough - and aggressively enough - to get burned. I felt an immediate kinship with him, and for a while, we shared common experiences and laughed. Eventually, after realizing

Two

how much time had passed, we hugged and agreed to stay in touch.

For the remainder of the evening, I walked around that room and initiated conversations with a procession of former classmates. Everyone was friendly and supportive. And it seemed that nearly all of us had been equally nervous about showing up there that night.

As the evening came to an end, I heard murmurs about afterparties and wondered if it made sense to tag along to one of them and continue in this revelry. With people rapidly dispersing and the hall nearly empty, I reconvened with my old pals Karol and Ray to discuss our next move.

Karol said she knew where one of the afterparties was and that we could walk there easily. So, the three of us headed into the silent streets of that warm June night, chatting about old times. We acknowledged how eerily familiar this moment felt. Years earlier, we'd spent countless nights wandering these empty streets.

When we got to the address Karol had been given for the afterparty, nobody answered the door. After waiting for a while and realizing no one was there, we laughed hysterically. Nothing had changed - so much time and life had passed, but we were still the weird misfit kids destined to wander these streets away from the crowd, laughing.

Eventually, the three of us decided it was time to call it a night, and I offered to drive Ray across town to the hotel he was staying at. He reluctantly accepted, and we said goodbye to Karol before getting into my little rental car.

A different kind of power

During our drive, Ray spoke about his life as a father and husband, sharing some of the joys and revelations he was experiencing on his journey. When I pulled into his hotel's parking lot, we shared a warm, heartfelt handshake and said goodbye.

In the wake of that night, I was overcome by a strange sense of belonging and confidence. For weeks leading up to the reunion, I was confused at how badly a part of me wanted to go and be there. To my mind, this seemed irrational and counterintuitive - a contradiction of every instinct I had as a teenager. But now, as I felt the aftereffects of being in that room with those peers, I was beginning to understand.

As a kid, I spent years walking through hallways and sitting in classrooms with those people feeling like a complete stranger - a weirdo, a loser, and a freak. But now, I'd returned to face that crowd once more. Instead of letting myself go numb and hide or close my heart (as I had in the past), I forced myself to say hello to the familiar faces and acknowledge the common threads of history and experience we shared. And when I did this - when I said hi, asked people how their lives had been, and told them how good it was to see them - I felt accepted. And who knows, maybe they did, too.

As simple as this was, it echoed through some deep place in me for weeks - a powerful healing tonic. The kid in me who, deep down, still felt like an oddity was

Two

shown that all those scary people he thought were so different from him weren't very different at all. Most of them felt just as vulnerable and self-conscious as he did. And, if he simply tried being nice to them, they were nice back.

The more I wandered around that room and spoke to those classmates, the more I heard a handful of common fears, hopes, and values echoed amongst their voices. One of these shared values was a deep appreciation for the quietness and simplicity of our hometown. Whether or not my classmates still lived there (most of them did), there was a near-unanimous love for that place's natural beauty and slow pace, and a set of simple ideals seemed to emerge from this.

I noticed a strange lack of materialism among that crowd. They wanted a good and meaningful life but nothing outrageous or grandiose. Maybe it was because of our age or where we came from, but this was not a group chasing fame and status. When I shared details of my humble existence as a server in a restaurant, not a single person batted an eyelid or exuded even a twinge of judgment. Some said they wished they could still be working as a waiter - sharing that waiting on tables had been the most fun they'd ever had while working a job. There was nothing but curiosity and acceptance of my choices.

All of this is to say that the more I spoke to those souls, the more I realized how incredibly similar we all were. I had also grown up to be a man who was not particularly materialistic. I developed a lifelong love for nature. And I felt as uncomfortable being there as everyone else did.

Given how much of an outsider I'd always seen myself as, this reality was mind-blowing. Sure, I was different in the ways that I was different. But the common ground we all shared was profound. As I let this in, I wondered how much of my identity was unique to me and how much of it had, in fact, been shaped by the place I came from - by the forests, rivers, mountains, and people I grew up in the company of. How much of *me* was actually formed by *them*? I couldn't say, but it was humbling to consider.

The strange new confidence I experienced in the aftermath of this event felt almost like a part of myself stuck in youthful insecurity finally came out of hiding. My anxieties were quieter than usual, and my heart was more stable and sure of itself.

As this was happening, I remembered the conversation I had with Marcus Fitzgerald on the night of the reunion. The two of us were bonding over our sometimes overzealous pursuit of self-improvement and healing when I said: "You know, Marcus, after years of inner work and spiritual exploration, it's moments like this that feel the scariest and most powerful. Coming back here and facing this social situation makes me shake like a child more than any spiritual work I've ever done."

"Yes!" Markus exclaimed. "Exactly. This is the work, Miles. We couldn't be anywhere more awkward right now, yet something pushed us to come here. This is the work."

Three

I was walking in the woods on a warm spring morning when a voice quietly whispered to me from the back of my mind. This hushed voice caught me off guard - not so much because of its spontaneous appearance in the silence of that moment, but because of what it said. It uttered a single, cryptic word: "Porn."

It didn't just say this word just once. As I continued my walk, it repeated itself again and again, whispering: "Porn. Porn. Porn…"

Confused and disturbed, I wondered why this word was suddenly echoing through my thoughts. It made no sense - I wasn't horny, I wasn't thinking about porn, and I didn't feel like watching it. Nothing whatsoever about that moment seemed like a time for porn. Dumbfounded, I continued walking, hoping to shrug off this strange intrusion into the peace of my solitude. But the voice didn't stop. As I wandered on, it continued whispering *porn*, and my confusion quickly turned to frustration.

A different kind of power

"I don't want to think about porn right now!" I said to myself. "This is not porn time - this is sacred communion with nature time."

For the rest of my outing, I tried to focus on the present moment and enjoy myself. But that voice remained, flickering in and out of my awareness, repeating itself like an unintelligible, perverted, broken record: "Porn. Porn. Porn…"

The following morning, when I went for a walk, this started again as soon as I entered the forest. That same subtle voice emerged in the silence, whispering: "Porn. Porn. Porn…"

Just like the previous day, there was that single word, nothing more. And it was whispered in a voice so subtle that I figured I was only noticing it because of how quiet, open, and receptive I had started to become during these walks.

That strange, repeating word was not accompanied by any sexual urge or fantasy. There were no visions or daydreams about pornographic imagery that arose with this voice - which made it all the more confusing. It was just the word porn bouncing around my head. Nothing more, nothing less.

I attempted once again to shift my awareness to the present moment. But the bizarre voice kept on whispering its simple, repetitive statement. No matter how hard I tried to ignore the voice or redirect my attention, it was there - and I was beginning to find it infuriating. I did not want to constantly think about porn.

Three

The voice returned unchanged when I went for my walk the following day. By now, I was realizing that this was not something I could simply shrug off or will out of existence, and I started to become more curious than upset. As the voice continued repeating itself in my head, I suspected that there might be something significant for me to understand here. So, instead of trying to ignore it, I began to explore the possible messages it might be trying to get through to me.

My first theory was that perhaps I should watch some porn. Maybe it would be good for me to get really into porn? It might help fill something that was missing from my life.

The moment I thought this, I got a sick feeling in my gut and decided that diving deep into the world of pornography probably wouldn't help anything.

Then, another possibility occurred to me: What if I had started going to such a wholesome and sacred place during these forest walks that something in my life totally inconsistent with that purity was surfacing for me to look at?

During this time, I was in the habit of watching porn somewhat regularly. I didn't consider it a problematic habit, as I never watched it compulsively and could go for periods without looking at it just fine. It wasn't something I felt proud of or excited about - but at some point, pornography crept into my life and became part of my mental environment. I was a single man who hadn't been with anyone in years, and I sometimes considered porn a form of sexual experience that might be better than casually hooking up with a person in real life. It was a safe, complication-free, virtual experience - all of which sounds miserable and depressing to say out loud. But, at the time, my logic seemed perfectly rational.

I knew porn came from a very troubled industry fuelled by the exploitation and dehumanization of vulnerable people. But it had become a part of my world. I was a guy on his lonesome, and it was a very easily attainable form of instant gratification. I knew it wasn't ideal, and I'd stopped watching it in the past, but never for good. Honestly, it just didn't seem like it was a big deal.

But now, as I was confronted by this troubling voice that would not stop echoing through my head, I began to suspect that my habit was so out of tune with the pure, ecstatic love I was stepping into every morning in the forest that something had to give. Maybe these two realities: The innocent experience of oneness with nature - and the heartbreaking world of modern pornography - were too conflicting to coexist peacefully within one mind. I couldn't be sure, but the longer I listened to that strange, repetitive voice from this angle, the more I felt I was on to something.

So, after some consideration, I decided it was time to stop watching porn and see what might happen. It may not help that voice go away, but it only made sense to give this a shot and test my theory - and I was confident that I would have no trouble letting porn go.

Three

My abstinence lasted three days. The habit of reaching out for instant gratification in that particular, potent form proved harder to shake than I had anticipated. But after I fell from grace and gave in to temptation, I picked myself up, dusted myself off, and renewed my commitment to staying away from porn. I suspected I would have no trouble letting it go for good this time.

I lasted approximately two days before faltering again. I was surprised by how much of a magnet porn had become for my attention and how difficult it was proving to be to actually walk away from.

There was also a compelling voice in my head that told me it didn't matter: *"Don't worry about this, Miles,"* it said. *"Porn is normal - everyone watches it. You don't have a problem with it. It's not ideal, but that's okay. Nobody's perfect! Just let yourself be human. You don't need to stop - it's fine."*

This voice was quite convincing and had won me over on many occasions. But this time, something was different. On my morning walks, I couldn't stop hearing that horrible word repeating in my head, and it was driving me crazy. On top of that, all of this forced me to do some soul-searching, and I realized that I really did not want to have porn in my life, mind, or emotional landscape anymore. It was over. I wanted it gone. But, as I watched myself repeatedly give in to its lure, I admitted that making a clean break was going to be more challenging than anticipated. It was an incredibly powerful temptation - being so immediately and effortlessly available. Porn, it turned out, was a formidable force.

Feeling committed to the challenge before me and humbled by my carnal, impulsive weakness, I was blessed by a sudden inspiration one afternoon while alone in my apartment: I opened up my laptop and started searching for long-form interviews with former porn stars. I figured that if I could hear enough true stories about the reality of what pornography was - from women who had been scarred by it - then maybe, just maybe, I could find the strength to say no to it.

The first video I found broke my heart. I listened in horror as a woman described being lured as an innocent girl to a modelling shoot in an exotic location, only to be picked up by a group of men, brought to an apartment, and taken advantage of in horrifying ways.

By some stroke of luck, this woman escaped from that ordeal alive. But she later discovered that hundreds of thousands of men had watched a video shared online of the worst moment of her life. It had been edited and uploaded to a popular, professional-looking porn site.

I sobbed as I listened to her - admiring the inconceivable courage it would have taken to simply go on after living after that, much less speak about it publicly.

One of the most troubling and shocking things about her story was that the video made from her experience

Three

was shared on a supposedly legitimate, professional porn platform. There was nothing consensual, appropriate, or legal about what had happened to her. Yet, it was published by what appeared to be a credible website. The implications of this were profound - it meant that no matter where one looked, the well of pornographic content was tainted with these types of traumatic experiences. As I wept at this woman's story, I knew the charade was over. There was no way I could watch porn with a clean conscience ever again, and I thought I might have finally found a way out: Hearing real people's lived experiences.

For the next week, I watched countless similar accounts from various women. Some of these interviews contained detailed stories of trauma, abuse, and trafficking. I heard the experiences of women who were victims of revenge porn, others who were recorded secretly without their knowledge or consent, and others still who had experienced forms of cruelty and humiliation that I had never heard of or imagined. I cried again and again. While I watched these interviews, I realized how incomprehensibly toxic the sea of online pornography is. And I felt absolute awe at each of those souls' courage to open up and share their stories with the world.

Several of those women said something chilling when they shared their accounts: They felt re-victimized by every man who watched a video of them. The gravity of those words burned into me, and it made complete sense.

A different kind of power

The brave women I listened to during this time became my teachers. I wanted to learn from them, hear their truth, and feel the actual human cost beneath the deceptive surface of this content. I hoped my brain would begin to rewire if I listened to enough of their stories. By filling myself with the heartbreaking reality, I hoped my conscience would build a firm footing in the harsh truth.

As this was happening, it dawned on me that the ecosystem of internet pornography had itself rewired my brain. The moment I visited a porn streaming site for the first time, I was bombarded by an endless sea of content that effectively normalized a reality that, up until that moment, I didn't even know existed. There were bizarre forms of hardcore sexuality flying at me from a thousand different directions - none of which resembled anything I'd ever seen on Earth. But the sheer volume of content reinforced a bizarre alternative reality in which things that appeared strange and disturbing were completely normal.

In this online reality, the awkward, vulnerable and tender human aspects of sex were nowhere to be seen. Nothing about it reflected my real-life experiences with women or my natural instincts and desires. I saw women being degraded, humiliated and disrespected constantly - and most confusing of all, acting like they enjoyed it. Things in this virtual world didn't make sense. But there was so much of it that I questioned my instincts. It did an excellent job of normalizing itself - functioning almost like a highly charismatic person who slowly convinced me: *This is normal stuff. This is perfectly*

Three

fine. Everybody is doing this - just look. Enjoy a little fun. Nothing is weird about this sea of people being filmed acting strange and having sex for millions of lonely men to stare at! And nothing's weird about being one of those lonely men.

Now, I was filling myself with a different reality - one that wasn't built on performance, lies, and manipulation. One that was devastating in its emotional truth and revealed the horrible ugliness behind the intoxicating facade of those sites and scenes.

With the stories and words of those women burning into me, my old habit was no longer an option. When I found myself alone in the evenings and felt the twitch of a familiar, comfortable desire come alive, I remembered those women, took a breath, and found something else to do.

It seemed that my health and wellness had not been a strong enough reason to tear myself away from this habit. I had known for years that watching porn was not good for my mental wellbeing - but I needed a reason that was bigger than that to keep me grounded when waves of temptation arrived. And that's what the voices of those women blessed me with. Because of them, I knew that if I chose to tap on my phone's screen and visit a particular site, I was directly supporting what had happened to them. Every click, every stream, and every page view generated some kind of ad revenue, however small, that kept that machine going.

And so, with my conscience fortified by the voices of those women, I stopped. But that strange voice in my head did not.

A different kind of power

My hope had been that as soon as I was no longer contaminating my mind with porn, the insidious, whispering voice that had been haunting me would disappear. In reality, it grew louder. After a week of abstinence, it became disturbingly loud during my morning walks. Where it had previously been a creepy hum that drifted in and out of my awareness, it was now a maddening shout, bouncing around my mind without restraint. Disturbed by this escalation, I wondered if I was mentally detoxing from porn, and this was one of my symptoms.

While this was happening, I also found myself overcome by a powerful desire to watch porn. Previously, consuming it had always seemed like a product of convenience. It was not something I aggressively sought out. It was just there, an endless library of sexual stimulation, free to watch with no effort. All it took was a click. This was a difficult temptation to resist - but I never dreamed or fantasized about it.

Yet now, as I wound down for bed every night, I felt an almost addictive urge. A primal impulse came from someplace deep inside me - a force of nature that felt almost uncontainable and was used to being fed with a specific, potent drug.

The power of this impulse shocked me, and it took all of my strength to resist its magnetic pull toward the satiating fix of watching just one video. Honestly, I don't think I had the strength to resist this temptation alone - the memory of those women carried me. Their stories were emblazoned in my mind. "Not happening, Miles,"

Three

I told myself. "Remember those women. It's not happening, ever."

Armed with that power, I could resist the temptation for another night.

The voice continued echoing through my head for an alarming amount of time, growing in intensity for weeks before slowly dimming and fading. It haunted the silence of my morning walks for months. Eventually, after it had faded significantly, I developed an appreciation for it and what it had revealed to me.

My surprising desire to watch porn also diminished during this time. It seemed to pass much more quickly than the voice, only lingering for a week or two before calming down and disappearing. It was an enormous relief to feel like I had broken free from this habit - though I knew it was still early days and anything could happen. All it would take was one moment of weakness, after all. The temptation was always there - a world of endless instant gratification waiting for me, just a click or a tap away.

But the further I got from that world, the more rooted I became in a new reason to stay away from it: I didn't want to hear that voice again. It was bizarre and, quite frankly, gross. I did not like the energy of porn reverberating through my psyche as it had been - and the haunting voice seemed to be just one symptom of that. I didn't want to feel possessed by a craving for something that I knew violated my deepest values as a human. And I didn't want to satisfy a primal, sacred yearning for connection with something so grim, unnatural, and unreal.

As that strange voice grew ever quieter in the absence of porn, something else began to happen that I did not expect: An emptiness or hunger grew in the vacant space porn used to fill in me - an intense longing that was honestly painful to feel. But, as uncomfortable as it was, something about it seemed very good. In the past, I'd used porn as a way of distracting myself from this void. Now, it was time to feel it. It was time to find another way of feeding this hunger. And I believed that having real-life experiences - almost any real-life experiences (provided they were healthy, respectful, and safe) - would be better than satiating it with a toxic virtual reality.

But instead of hopping back on the dating apps and finding someone to hook up with, I was pulled in a different direction: I began to work on creative projects with more focus. I spent more time outdoors. There was a rush of life energy I hadn't anticipated that quickly translated into a reservoir of motivation to live, explore, work, and achieve.

As the weeks passed, I also began to feel a renewed sense of innocence. It's difficult to describe, but as I walked through the forest, not only did that repetitive

Three

voice grow increasingly quiet, but a feeling of love, hope, and tenderness took its place.

This wasn't an altogether unfamiliar feeling, but it was stronger now. It felt like I was getting something vital in myself back. I thought about the stories of those women - then about the adult videos I'd watched habitually and how a pure, innocent part of me must have felt crushed by the tragedy of this world. How could a tender, sacred inner child remain open to life when he was being bombarded by such a gruesome reality? How could he not become cynical and hopeless when he was witnessing the desecration of innocence and being told it was normal?

As I felt a hopeful, bright, and wholesome part of my heart come back online, the seriousness of my predicament became all the more apparent. That voice had been relentless because I needed to understand something. It had repeated its single, cryptic word because I needed to get porn out of my life, mind, and spirit - to get something sacred back.

I'd thought it was such a trivial thing, but the more time passed, the more convinced I was that this might have been one of the most significant decisions of my adult life.

Then, one day during a walk in the forest, when I heard the word "Porn" whispered in a hushed voice at the back of my mind, I found myself spontaneously completing that statement by adding: "...does not belong in my life." The next time I heard that word in my head, I spontaneously finished the sentence again: "Porn... is not part of my world."

A different kind of power

Suddenly, a strange, uncontrollable intrusion became an affirmation - a statement of values, choices, and needs. Porn had a new meaning and a different context. It was no longer something that floated freely without boundaries in my life.

About six months after I stopped watching porn, I decided I wanted to share the experience I'd had on my podcast. It was a profoundly impactful choice that reverberated through my life in positive ways. Because of this, I felt more enthusiastic to talk about it than almost anything else.

After some planning and reflection, I recorded a straightforward account of my experience, then uploaded and shared the finished product with the world. Given that I had already spent years writing and publishing intensely personal and vulnerable stories, it surprised me how ashamed and embarrassed I felt immediately after posting this podcast. Something about it was scarier than anything else.

After all, I was talking publicly about me watching porn and having a hard time stopping. That alone made me sweat. But I felt this was an important subject to discuss openly, particularly for young men. So, I accepted my pain and embarrassment as a personal sacrifice.

Typically, when I published a new podcast, I shared it on social media so anyone interested could check it

Three

out. I knew a handful of readers, friends, coworkers, and acquaintances listened to my podcast regularly. But when I went to share this episode, I seized up in shame. I knew that nearly everyone I worked with would see this, and the discomfort of that was almost too much to bear. But, as crippling as my fear of judgment was, I knew what I had to do - I let my ego suffer and shared it.

After doing this, I turned off my phone and continued with my day, trying to avoid meditating on how my coworkers and others might perceive me. But when I had to go to work that afternoon, the awkwardness was inescapable.

As I arrived at the restaurant, I walked into the back with my head hung low, wishing I could be invisible. I knew that most of my coworkers had probably seen the subject of my new podcast, and some of them had almost certainly listened to it.

"It's over," I thought. "I'm done. This was too much, too personal - nobody will understand. They're gonna think I'm a creep. I'm a dead man."

The first person I saw there was my manager Karla (who I knew followed my podcast). We exchanged a quick hello and nothing more as she rushed into her office. I was sweating bullets.

Walking onto the restaurant floor, I sheepishly said hello to two of my female coworkers, feeling the sting of shame as it coursed through me. Then, as I readied myself for a busy shift, another one of my coworkers - a young man named Frank - approached me: "Hey,

Miles," he said quietly, "I listened to an episode of your podcast."

"Which one?" I asked, curious where this was going.

"Ummm, your most recent one," Frank replied nervously.

"Oh, the one about porn?" I blurted out loud - before realizing Frank was more embarrassed to be talking about this subject than I was.

"Uhh - yeah," he confirmed in an anxious whisper.

We walked somewhere a bit quieter, and I asked: "What did you think?"

"It was pretty interesting," he replied. "I actually wanted to ask you some questions about what you went through, but I don't know - maybe when there isn't anyone around."

I understood his desire for privacy (having just completely destroyed my own), and we agreed to reconvene when the time was right.

A few minutes later, Frank decided to continue our conversation, asking for details regarding my story and sharing his concerns and thoughts. I was an open book, telling him everything I'd been going through over the past months. I reassured Frank there was nothing wrong with him and nothing weird about any of his struggles - we never evolved to live with these kinds of technological temptations. And that meant we each needed to develop our own power to live among them without being devoured.

"The biggest surprise for me," I shared, "is how much letting go of this has influenced the rest of my life. I have been doing more creative work, getting out and

Three

trying new things, and feeling a hunger for life that I haven't felt in such a long time. It's been really beautiful - totally life-changing."

Frank was quietly receptive, and we talked about our shared experiences for a while. Regardless of what he chose to do with himself after that conversation, I came away from it with a gift: For all of my shame and embarrassment, one person received something that helped them feel less alone. That was more than enough.

Four

In late spring, I had the first in a series of vivid dreams. During this dream, I was walking through a forest filled with massive, stunning wild Reishi mushrooms. The bodies of these mushrooms were a glistening deep red, growing from tree trunks and branches in various strange, exaggerated, saucer-like shapes. They were larger than any mushroom I had ever seen or knew existed on Earth and exuded a spectacular, magical aura. Walking deep into the forest, I stared in awe at these otherworldly life forms as they grew above and around me.

Then, I thought to myself: "Isn't this a bit early in the year for Reishi mushrooms?"

At that moment, I woke up. As I lay in bed, something about that dream seemed significant.

The previous year, I'd discovered Reishi mushrooms growing in various local forests and developed a deep fascination with them. It was wonderful to see those

A different kind of power

beautiful life forms again, even if it was just in my sleep. I quickly forgot about that dream as I got out of bed and prepared for the day.

During my walk later that morning, I was deep in thought as I strolled along a forest trail and something in the distance caught my attention: A tiny speck of bright, glowing white registered in my peripheral vision. When I looked up and saw the source of this bright colour, I couldn't believe my eyes. I climbed across several fallen logs and jumped over a small stream to investigate more closely.

When I arrived within a few feet of this curiosity, my initial suspicion was confirmed: I'd found the beginnings of a fresh, young Reishi mushroom growing from the base of a rotting tree trunk. Its surface was mostly bright white - so bright that it stood out in stark contrast to the muted earth tones of the surrounding forest. It had a small patch of shiny, scarlet red near its base that would grow larger in time.

I knelt down and stared in awe at this mushroom's elegant, smooth, almost alien form - and thought to myself that it was surprisingly early in the year to find a Reishi mushroom. At that moment, I remembered the dream from the previous night, and my jaw dropped.

I stayed there for the next few minutes and silently studied this extraordinary little mushroom. I had no interest in harvesting it, but something about its existence there absorbed me - the same way those Reishi mushrooms in my dream had. And whatever mystical power the dream mushrooms had appeared to emanate,

Four

this real-life version possessed in equal or greater measure.

When I finally continued on my way, I struggled to process what I'd just seen - and the strange dream that preceded (and mirrored) this encounter. Somehow, it all felt very significant.

The previous fall, I harvested a large Reishi mushroom while hiking in a remote forested area near the mountains. When I brought it home, I cut that mushroom into thin slices and dried it for future use as a medicinal tea. Since then, however, I'd shied away from experimenting with consuming any of it. This was partly due to fear surrounding my expertise (or lack thereof) in mushroom identification. I'd done plenty of due diligence and was nearly one hundred percent certain that what I had harvested and dried was a Reishi mushroom (and therefore safe). But I still worried that I could have been wrong, and I didn't want to take any risks. The slightest possibility of error in my identification was enough to scare me away from consuming any of the dried mushroom. Over time, I grew content letting my little stash of dehydrated Reishi sit in the cupboard, with no idea when or if I would ever gather the courage and motivation to use it.

But in the days after that vivid dream and the surprise morning encounter that followed it, a familiar voice began to nudge me toward action. And this voice,

A different kind of power

while very familiar, was not one that I would expect to encourage me to experiment with wild-harvested, medicinal mushrooms. It was the voice of my Granny, who had passed away over fifteen years earlier.

I loved my Granny dearly, and during this time, I had been reflecting on her presence and importance in my life. She had been a stern disciplinarian who, when I was a child, seemed to always be watching for opportunities to teach her grandchildren about manners, being proper, and acting with integrity. Granny was a ballbuster. If a *please* or a *thank you* was ever forgotten at the end of a sentence, she would snap into action with a lacerating: "I beg your pardon?" Her presence demanded a certain calibre of behaviour.

Now, as an adult, when I found myself in seemingly inconsequential moments of moral transgression, my Granny's voice would often come into my head to keep me in line. For example, during a shift at work, I might be dropping off a stack of dirty plates at the dish pit, and while putting them down for sorting and cleaning, accidentally drop a paper napkin on the floor. Noticing the tiny mess I made, I would think to myself: "Who cares? Nobody is going to notice that - and it's not going to bother anyone if they do notice. It'll get swept up at the end of the night with all the other debris people have dropped."

Then, Granny's voice would appear, with its trademark disciplinarian tone: "Excuse me, young man?"

That's all I needed to hear. I would stop whatever I was doing, bend down, and clean up after myself (or, in

Four

many cases, clean up after someone else - if that was what the situation called for). Granny's voice was too strong and intimidating to ignore. And honestly, I welcomed and loved it. The older I got, the more I could appreciate how that part of my Granny had been a blessing to me. Her discipline and demand for propriety were things I now carried within me as a man, and they were wonderful gifts. Hearing her voice at the back of my mind - like a distinct branch of my conscience - was always beautiful, even though it almost always meant doing more work for no personal gain.

But now, I suddenly heard her voice sending a very different message than usual. Rather than being a clear part of my conscience telling me to do the right thing, no matter how insignificant or invisible, it was telling me something confusing: "Drink your tea."

Over several days, I began to hear my Granny's voice ever more frequently, repeating this simple message with maternal gravity: "Drink your tea, young man. Drink your tea." Somehow, it was obvious that the *tea* being referred to was the Reishi I had dried and stored for this purpose the previous fall.

My initial reaction was shock and disbelief that my Granny's voice was urging me towards this wild mushroom medicine. But as this continued, it started to make sense.

Throughout my days, this message consistently flashed through my thoughts with my grandmother's unflinching intensity: *Drink your tea*. As I continued to hear it, I sensed that drinking my tea was akin to eating a bowl of hearty chicken soup - an old-time, simple folk remedy that strengthened and healed.

My resistance to drinking this tea was surprisingly strong. But I continued to hear the message, whether in quiet moments of reflection or while rushing around a restaurant with a tray of cocktails balanced on my hand.

Then, the dreams came. I started seeing Reishi mushrooms in my dreams nearly every night - often in strange cosmic or mystical settings. And soon, for reasons I did not understand, it began to feel like the single most critical thing for me to do was drink that tea.

In my mind, the most important things for me to do at that moment were to market my new book, sell countless copies of it, and finally start dating women again. In my gut, however, only one thing seemed relevant or urgent: *Drink your tea.*

So, after months of avoidance and hesitation, I opened my cupboard and removed the plastic bag of dried, wild-harvested Reishi I'd tucked away there. I took a handful of crisp, dehydrated mushroom slices from it and diced them into tiny pieces before placing them into a slow cooker, covering them with plenty of water, and brewing up a strong batch of tea.

The resulting broth was a dull amber colour and had a rich mushroom aroma. After pouring a mug of this liquid and letting it cool, I took my first sip. It tasted delicious - slightly bitter with a complex earthy flavour. Something about drinking it was highly evocative - like consuming a broth of forest spirits that immediately

Four

transported my imagination to the immense, lush place of natural power that this mushroom came from.

As I sipped it, I thought: "This tastes like a forest goddess." And I wondered what effect, if any, it might have on me.

Once I made that initial batch of tea, I began a daily ritual of consuming a mug of the brew. It could have been my imagination, but it seemed that the effects of it were immediate and pronounced: I noticed a deep, unusual sense of calm, stability, and inner peace. As I ingested this mushroom and my body responded to it, I felt that it was (at least in my unique case) slightly consciousness-altering. Its mind-altering properties, however, were quite unlike those of traditional psychedelic mushrooms. In my limited experience with hallucinogenic mushrooms, they tended to bend, distort, and destabilize my awareness - often magnifying anxieties and spinning my perception wildly off from its normal foundations. As I continued my daily practice of drinking this tea, however, Reishi appeared to be doing something entirely different: It stabilized, grounded, and strengthened me. I found myself less emotionally reactive - unfazed by the little things that could easily bother me but that I knew didn't matter.

There was a notable shift in my perception of the most significant source of stress in my world at that

A different kind of power

moment: A painful lack of self-confidence that publishing my new book had triggered. Having still only sold a handful of copies of that book, I'd been living with a constant background noise of negativity and self-criticism. But suddenly, that noise went quiet.

It was as though this tea bestowed a strength that fit me and my situation perfectly. A part of my spirit that had felt crushed by the material conditions of my life as a writer suddenly didn't care. There was a deeper connection to my heart and its wisdom - a sense that if I had done my best and given my all, that's all there was to do. Having strangers accept me and pat me on the back didn't matter - the work was done either way.

When a coworker asked me how I was doing one day at the restaurant during this time, I gushed effusively about the wild medicinal mushroom I'd harvested and made into tea, and how it was helping me.

"Does it get you high?" she asked, sincerely curious.

"Well, not in a normal sense," I replied. "I feel more balanced, calm, and stable - so it's almost the opposite of a psychedelic trip. But I feel very alive - like the reality of my heart is easier to access. My anxious thoughts aren't as loud as usual, and I feel more connected to my inner power. It's as though I have help from an ally."

"I need that!" she exclaimed, and our other nearby coworkers echoed her sentiment.

As I continued drinking this tea, my Reishi dreams intensified, further contributing to my fascination with this fungus. I started researching some of the traditional

Four

wisdom and lore around Reishi, eager to understand what I was experiencing. I found many descriptions of its general, well-recognized, beneficial properties: It was reported to support the immune system, help manage stress and anxiety and calm the mind, along with many other positive effects.

I was already familiar with much of this information, but given the marked reduction in stress and emotional volatility that I was experiencing, it took on new meaning.

More than anything, I wanted to know if there was a clear record of its use as a spiritual tool. It did not take much digging before I found some information that satisfied my curiosity: According to the Wikipedia entry for Reishi, in ancient Taoist China, Reishi mushrooms (called Ling Zhi) were considered "spirit mushrooms" and a concentrated, hallucinogenic decoction was made from them for spiritual purposes. To quote from the text cited in that entry, this brew gave individuals "the opportunity to see spirits, or become spirits themselves by receiving the magical energy of the immortal xians, located on the 'fields of grace' in the heavenly 'mushrooms fields.'"

As I read on, I discovered that Reishi had been part of a rich and storied ancient spiritual tradition, with several mentions of it being used to produce a psychoactive, shamanic brew. These references all seemed vague, were translated into archaic, unclear language, and remained mysterious to me. They also referred to numerous Asian forms of Reishi, not the variety that grew in my area. But they provided a

A different kind of power

glimmer of context and validation relative to what I was experiencing. I did feel more connected to the spirit world on Reishi. There was an unmistakable spiritual power I felt being nourished in me.

As I continued to drink my tea, the days grew longer and warmer, and my bag of dried Reishi quickly diminished. The tiny Reishi mushroom I'd found growing on a rotting tree trunk in late spring developed into a large, stunning specimen. And I found many more of those mushrooms growing elsewhere. I observed all of them with joy and felt very rich to be in contact with a world so holy and beautiful.

One evening during this time, my friend Dane called. We spoke for a few minutes about his life, and then I asked him if he'd had a chance to look at the copy of my new book I'd sent him in the mail. Dane became noticeably uncomfortable when I brought this subject up, saying very little but communicating multitudes through the strained awkwardness of his tentative words.

"Ahhh, I actually read the whole thing," he said nervously, sounding like he wished he could be anywhere else talking about any other subject.

"Well, what did you think?" I asked, sincerely curious.

Four

There was a moment of silence before he replied: "Oh man. Oh man, this is hard - but I have to be honest..."

At that moment, I realized what was about to occur, and something miraculous happened inside me. Dane was an old friend, and in the past, I had valued his perspective and critical feedback regarding my writing very highly. He'd even helped me a great deal with editing one of my previous books, and I was deeply indebted to him for that. While writing this book, however, my gut told me not to show it to Dane or discuss it with him. I didn't question that instinct and decided to wait until it was done and published before sharing it with him. Now, hearing the discomfort in my friend's voice, I knew what was coming.

"Okay," he continued. "Well, your writing is very... professional. Like, I think it's more professional than ever. So, that's great. But - as your friend, I have to be honest. And the book... it doesn't seem like it works. You know?"

I asked him to explain his thoughts further and quietly listened.

"It's just - maybe it's too experimental for me. I couldn't get into it. And there were a couple of points where I wanted to throw the book at a wall, I was so annoyed. And the ending - oh, it drove me crazy!"

He honestly and graciously shared his reservations and criticisms of the book before adding: "You know, I'd like to see a little more analysis of the stories you tell. Like, if you could interpret your experiences a bit more..."

"The whole point is that I don't interpret the experiences," I said. "The whole spirit of the book is centred around me not trying to figure things out, find easy answers, or fix myself."

"Okay," he continued, "I just feel like I need to say this because I care about you - and I think if you rewrote it, it could be a lot better. It could be the same book, just rewritten to clarify what you're getting at - more analysis and clearer teaching. More like a classic self-help book."

It was at this moment that I realized something phenomenal was happening. As my wonderful, well-meaning friend critiqued my art, I stayed calm. This conversation would have crushed me in the past - a good friend's critical perceptions would have shattered my fragile conviction in my work. I would have clung to his words, losing my centre of gravity and sense of self. The shame would have nearly knocked me out - and it would have taken days for my nervous system to begin recovering.

But, at that moment, I was calm. I politely - with a bit of passion and defensiveness - disagreed with my friend. I told him there was no chance of me completely rewriting the book. It was my baby, and it had already been born. And now, as the parent of this baby, it was my duty to love, accept, and protect it - regardless of its imperfections or what others thought.

As I finished saying this, I stared out my apartment window at the dark, cloudy night, and a flash of lightning illuminated the entire sky. My eyes widened, and I wondered if the heavens were flickering as a way

Four

of rejoicing about what had just happened: I listened to someone else's strong perspective - and I didn't let it consume or destroy mine. I saw where my friend was coming from - and while I respected his intentions and differing taste, I disagreed. In the past, I would have easily let another's beliefs and feelings trample my own, but this time, something was different.

As I registered the uncanny timing of that lightning strike, I thought to myself: *It's the Reishi. I have its strength.*

We continued speaking, and Dane kindly implored me to consider what he was saying. He was clearly well-intentioned and just wanted his friend to succeed. But my conviction didn't budge. At that moment, it seemed infinitely more important to believe in the authenticity of what I'd done than to change it for the tastes of others - or to fit into a marketplace.

As we continued to speak, I shared: "I think it's just not your cup of tea - and that's awesome! It's so beautiful to understand that I can't create something that every type of person will love. Accepting that feels like the ultimate freedom."

For so long, I'd sought approval from others like a child looking up to his parents - believing that if I could win their acceptance, I would be winning at life. In reality, the less I cared about gaining their approval, the more freely I could live.

Dane and I spoke for another hour or so, eventually arriving at a place of mutual understanding and respect. I marvelled at my strange state of equanimity. It was as though I'd just been given another person's confidence

A different kind of power

to try on and walk around in. When we got off the phone, I sat down and remembered the urgency with which I'd been compelled to *"drink your tea."* It was beginning to make sense.

After a brief period of inner peace and stability, something very disappointing happened: The mushrooms stopped working. Over several days, I was overcome by waves of sadness, frustration, and irritability that grew in strength until it seemed like whatever gift that tea had blessed me with disappeared. As my supply dwindled, I continued consuming my daily dose. Yet, I began to feel more volatile and moody than I had in ages for no apparent reason. After experiencing that short window of inner peace, I couldn't understand why I suddenly felt so overwhelmed by emotion.

Then, I had another dream: In it, I was walking through an open, rocky desert landscape beneath a clear, star-filled night sky. I saw several coyotes at the top of a ridge near me. Curious to know what they were doing, I climbed toward them. When I got close, I could see that they were playing with Reishi mushrooms. The mushrooms they had were glowing in various bright, neon colours - and the Coyotes were eating them and proceeding to light up and glow like the mushrooms, then shoot into the sky - flying across the desert as though they were projected out of a cannon. This

Four

appeared to be great fun for the Coyotes - they were laughing and treating their activity like a humorous and exhilarating game enabled by the magical power of their luminescent mushrooms.

When I woke up, a singular thought flashed into my mind: *The Reishi is still working. I'm feeling messed up because it's still working. It's just doing something I didn't expect. It's playing with me.*

After that night, I continued drinking my tea but let go of any rigid expectations around what I thought it should be doing to me. I suspected that, like the mythological symbol of the Coyote (the sacred trickster), it might work in ways I could not understand. It might be playfully stirring things up in me that my mind thought were bad to feel - but that were somehow beneficial.

As spring gave way to summer, the various Reishi mushrooms I'd first spotted earlier in the season grew into large, gorgeous, fully mature specimens. My morning walks stretched longer as I found more and more of these mushrooms and repeatedly visited them, silently observing their remarkable daily growth - possessed by an obsessive fascination.

After I ran out of dried mushroom to brew tea from, I felt satisfied simply being close to these lifeforms as they grew in nature. Being near them had a strong effect on me - as though I was still very much drinking my tea.

Weeks passed, and I observed new tiny protrusions of white flesh grow into large crimson-red saucers throughout the woods, never harvesting any of the mushrooms I studied. For now, witnessing them was enough. It felt like I was learning something about creation by seeing how they grew. I couldn't (and can't) put what I was learning into words - but I became convinced that through this intimacy and observation, I was receiving some kind of wisdom from nature. When I saw a fresh Reishi growing from an old rotting tree trunk, I often felt that I was looking at something more akin to a spirit than an earthly being.

I returned to watch them grow often, a humble student completely infatuated with his teacher and happy to spend countless hours in that open-air classroom with them. My fascination pushed me to explore many wild and forested areas near the city, searching for more of these remarkable beings. When I had a day off from work during this time, it was normal for me to go to a new hiking trail - curious if I might encounter any of these beautiful fungi. My intention was, at some point, to harvest some to use as tea, but I was not in any rush. As I discovered more of them, I approached the possibility of picking them with the same kind of patience, discernment, and tenderness that I had learned to apply to dating or searching for a mate: There was no rush. And before we even touched, it needed to feel right. If it didn't feel like a complete yes,

Four

it was a no. And simply being around them, without anything physical coming from it, was extraordinary.

Then, one day, I went to see some mushrooms I'd been watching grow for almost a month and found that all of them had been harvested. Apparently, someone else appreciated these beautiful beings, too, and took every single one of them. As I continued my walk, I discovered that many of the other mushrooms I'd been watching grow had also been harvested.

I felt a mixture of rage and sadness - but was also unsurprised. I'd seen this happen before and knew people liked to harvest these mushrooms for personal and commercial use. To my astonishment, they sometimes appeared to take every last one they saw. And while it sickened an innocent part of me that something so beautiful and sacred could be taken away so abruptly, I knew this was the reality of people and the world.

Seeing others do this almost made me question my own conscience. When I went to see a patch of mushrooms, I wondered if I should let go of my hesitations and just harvest them. After all, if someone else was going to ruthlessly take them all, why shouldn't I take them for myself? It would make no difference in the end.

But I couldn't do it. My gut continued telling me to not harvest any of them, and I listened. Letting the actions of others erode my conscience felt like the most foolish thing I could do. So, instead, I leaned further into my natural instincts. I continued to enjoy those mushrooms as a witness and admirer and accepted that others would be guided differently. When I saw a patch of them that I'd been watching grow stripped bare by someone, I was not tempted to do the same, and I had no regrets. It had been a blessing to witness that miracle of creation. What felt right to me and what felt right to someone else might have been very different. And it was more important for me to listen to that feeling than to disown it so I could be like others or have what they had.

For the next two months, much of my time revolved around exploring forests, finding mushrooms, and drinking in their beauty. As this continued, I experienced an ongoing high from simply being around them. I felt euphoric, blissed out, and deeply infatuated with nature and life.

When the nights grew longer and colder, and the first signs of summer's departure were obvious, I found myself momentarily sobering up from the high I'd been riding for months - and suddenly wondered what the hell I'd just done with a significant period of time. In my head, this was supposed to have been a highly productive season. I had a new book I was supposed to be marketing relentlessly and a completely neglected goal of dating women and finding a partner. But throughout this summer, I didn't care about any of that.

I'd been selling an average of two or three books a month during this period - a number that should have

Four

been a savage, horrifying disappointment. But given the reality I'd been infusing myself with, I didn't care. I didn't even see this as a negative outcome - from a certain perspective, it seemed perfect. The blissed-out, forest-wandering perspective said: *You're growing more this way. You're being forced to believe in yourself when the world doesn't reassure you - and that's the ultimate freedom.*

While I couldn't help but shake my head and wonder if I'd completely squandered a chunk of life by stumbling around local forests like a stoner on a natural high, I sensed something important was transpiring through all this. It felt like part of me was being revived. Those long walks in local forests were facilitating some kind of deep healing. And while I had nothing superficial to show for this season of wandering, I believed it was restoring a power in me that I needed.

Five

I had been living down the hall from my neighbour Stanley for two years before we had our first conversation. This meeting took place in the spring of 2020, during the initial weeks of the pandemic lockdown. After spending an ungodly amount of time in technology-distracted isolation, I went outside for a much-needed walk in the park. I found some welcome reprieve from the anxieties and stagnation of my apartment in the sunshine and fresh ocean air. Near the end of my walk, I stopped by a set of outdoor pull-up bars near the beach for a quick workout. With my gym closed due to public health restrictions, this equipment was an ideal alternative, and I began to visit it regularly.

On this occasion, several other men arrived and started working out alongside me. Under normal circumstances, I wouldn't have exchanged more than a polite hello or a silent nod with these strangers. But given the strange instability and confusion of that moment, something else naturally happened. As we took breaks between sets of push-ups, pull-ups, and dips, we acknowledged how bizarre everything happening in the world was.

Standing feet away from an athletic young man I'd seen working out at those bars numerous times, I asked: "How have you been doing with all of this, brother?"

He sighed before answering: "Oh man, it's been weird. My family is all overseas in Nigeria. So, you know, it's been pretty lonely. I'm scared for the people I love and starting to go crazy from too much time on my own…"

I nodded and shared my similar experience. For the next hour, I slowly went through my workout, taking regular breaks to talk with a handful of other men I'd seen before and never spoken to as they came and went. The collective vulnerability of that moment seemed to have opened something up in us - we were so uncertain of everything that the illusory differences and barriers that typically separated us were gone. It was beautiful, and my heart soaked in the nourishment of these fleeting conversations. After leaving, I walked home with the excitement of a kid who'd made some new schoolyard friends - overjoyed and straining to remember the names of the kind strangers I'd just encountered.

When I returned to my apartment building, I walked into the lobby and saw an elderly neighbour I'd crossed paths with countless times. As with those young men at the pull-up bars, I had never said anything more than a cordial hello to this neighbour. But this day, something was different. The world had stopped, and neither of us

Five

had anywhere to go. So, after exchanging a greeting, we lingered and struck up a conversation.

I asked my neighbour how he was weathering the isolation and confusion of the moment. His response was surprisingly measured and calm - almost serene: "Oh, I'm just fine," he softly said. "It's a little different not being able to go and visit friends, but all things considered, I'm doing very well. I've got my health, so there isn't too much for me to worry about. I have no complaints."

We spoke for a while about how we were trying to keep ourselves busy, and I learned that, like me, my neighbour lived alone. I was touched by how optimistic and unfazed he was by the disruption and uncertainty of the moment. I did not know his age, but he walked slowly and patiently with the assistance of a cane and might have been considered someone who was at high risk for the mystery illness that had brought the world to a halt. Yet he didn't seem worried about it. His presence was peaceful and warm.

After talking for some time, we formally introduced ourselves, and I learned that my neighbour's name was Stanley. When we said goodbye and went our separate ways, the childlike sense of excitement I had felt on my walk home multiplied in strength. I couldn't believe it - I just met *another* beautiful person. And, just like those guys at the pull-up bars, this was someone I'd seen countless times before. He was someone I never would have imagined to be so kind, warm, and interesting. And all it took to discover that was a simple *Hi, how are you?*

A different kind of power

Bursting with excitement, I stepped into my apartment, found a piece of paper on my desk, and wrote down my neighbour's name so I wouldn't forget it, scribbling: MET STANLEY TODAY.

After that initial conversation with Stanley, I began to say hello to him every time we crossed paths, and occasionally stopped to ask how he was doing. Initially, these interactions were brief and straightforward. But over time, there was a familiarity and warmth that grew in them. I often saw Stanley sitting on a bench or resting on a ledge as I walked to the grocery store down the street from our building. Sometimes, he would be chatting with a friend or acquaintance. At other times, he would simply be watching the river of humanity as it flowed by. When he was alone, I would cross the street to say hello and ask him how life was going. Often, he would answer: "Oh, I can't complain," in his gentle voice before sharing what he had been up to. The more I got to know Stanley, the more that answer, *I can't complain*, seemed to be emblematic of his personality.

Stanley told me one day that he needed hip surgery. But, given his age, his doctors had advised him that he may not survive such an invasive and traumatic procedure. So, instead of risking his life for a possible improvement to his mobility, he decided to resign himself to the limitations of his aging body.

Five

"It could be worse," he gently told me. "I can still get out and about and do everything I need to. It's a little hard sometimes, but I'm a very lucky person. I can't complain."

There were those words again: *I can't complain.*

Of course, Stanley could have complained. He could have chosen from an endless list of challenges and grievances to legitimately complain about. During one of our conversations, I pointed this out.

"I think you actually could complain, Stanley. And it would be very reasonable. We're living in a world of able-bodied, well-fed, and privileged individuals who rarely stop complaining about trivial, superficial things. That you, of all people, don't have any complaints - given the very real challenges of your life - is remarkable."

Stanley thought for a moment before responding: "Well now, that's true. But you know," he said slowly and deliberately, "I have always just felt like a lucky person."

Over several years, my appreciation for Stanley's presence steadily grew. He gradually became a significant pillar of my world - the same way that the forested nature park I walked in every morning was. When I strolled through my little neighbourhood, it was always a pleasure to see Stanley sitting at a street corner, slowly drinking a coffee and watching the world go by. Every conversation with him felt like a gift - an interaction with someone special, someone far different from all the other people I interacted with day to day.

A different kind of power

At one point, I gave Stanley a copy of a book I wrote during the pandemic lockdowns, and he read it cover to cover. When I asked him what he thought of it, his words were simple, warm, and sincere: "It was really interesting, Miles. I really enjoyed it. You've certainly lived a very fascinating life…"

We didn't speak much about the book's details, but his words of support and kindness were deeply appreciated. He often asked me if I was writing anything else, and when I did eventually start to work on my next book, he made sure to inquire how it was going every time we saw one another, sharing that he was very much looking forward to reading it once it was done.

When the day came that the book was published, Stanley was one of the first people I gave a copy to. After reading it, he again shared words of support and encouragement with me. I was grateful for his kindness and perspective.

A month or two after giving Stanley that latest book, I was on my way to the grocery store. My mind was buzzing with anxieties about this new work being poorly received and not selling more copies yet, when I saw Stanley walking slowly toward me in the distance. The moment I laid eyes on him, the pettiness and superficiality of my worries became obvious. Something about Stanley's mere presence put things into perspective and unmasked my concerns, exposing their childish nature.

It might have been that I saw a ninety-two-year-old man patiently walking, ever so slowly, with a cane -

Five

stopping to rest on the cement ledge of an apartment building's front planter without a shred of frustration or resentment in his heart - and it revealed something.

When I arrived at his side, I said: "You know, Stanley, sometimes I worry about the dumbest things. I'm so lucky just to be alive. And when I see you - a man who could complain about so much and who I never hear being negative about anything - it helps me remember what matters. You always seem happy to be here. It's an incredible example for all of us, Stanley. I really mean that."

"Well," he responded, "that's very nice of you."

For the next twenty minutes, we spoke about life, and at one point, I asked Stanley how he managed to stay so positive.

"Well, I do have a problem with negative people," he replied. "Some people only see the bad in life and complain about everything. I don't have much patience for that. It actually really bothers me. I have to keep away from those people."

"That makes sense," I responded. "It can be contagious, can't it?"

"Well, yes, I think it can. It's one thing that really bothers me."

After that conversation, I often remembered Stanley during moments of frustration and negativity. The mere thought of my elder neighbour could sometimes act like a tonic - calming the short-sighted, impatient voices in my head. There was something about Stanley that just had that effect. He exuded a wisdom that was beyond words. It was part of his presence, who he was. An

A different kind of power

accumulation of human experience and grace simply emanated from his person. In a world filled with men posturing as teachers and authorities in dubious ways, Stanley was a rare and sacred thing: A calm elder with no pretensions, nothing to prove, and no bullshit.

I often saw Stanley sitting on street corners, talking with neighbours, acquaintances, or old friends. Over time, as I observed more and more people sitting and talking with Stanley, I realized that I was not alone in my admiration for this man. A vast network of people loved him and appreciated his presence in their world. In this sense, Stanley appeared to be a very rich person. There was nothing fancy or flashy about him. His home was in our old apartment building, he wore humble clothing and lived by himself. He had no wife or children. But it was clear that across his decades of life, his warm, curious, and welcoming heart had established an abundance of wealth in its highest and most refined form: Sincere human connection.

As we got to know one another better, Stanley periodically brought up a specific theme during our conversations: My singlehood.

On one occasion, he remarked: "You've got to find yourself a girlfriend, Miles. I think you're really going to enjoy it when you find the right person."

In response, I awkwardly laughed and said: "You're right. I'm going to get out there. It's just... I've been busy with life. And honestly, I feel filled with love from so many different places - there isn't the same pressure to find it in a single person anymore."

Five

Stanley quietly nodded, accepting my excuse before reminding me that I still needed to take a leap out of my shell at some point.

As the weather began to get colder in late fall, I noticed that I was seeing Stanley less and less. And though I couldn't be sure if it was just my imagination, whenever I did see him, he seemed a bit out of breath - a little more worn down than usual. It was a subtle thing, but I took note of it, and it pushed me to make sure, more than ever, that I let Stanley know how much I appreciated him. Sometimes, I would tell him, truthfully, that it was the highlight of my day to cross his path. He had become a beacon of light in my world, and I couldn't let that go unacknowledged.

One morning, I was returning home from a long walk when I decided to take an unusual route back into my building. I always came and went through the front entrance - but the previous day, I spotted some Amanita Muscaria mushrooms (the iconic red-capped, white polka-dotted mushrooms of fairytales and folklore) growing near my building's side door. As I approached the spot where I'd seen those otherworldly mushrooms, I walked past the side entrance at the very moment someone opened it up. I turned and saw Stanley in the doorway, appearing somewhat disoriented, with two men helping him as he moved much more slowly than usual.

A different kind of power

I said hello, and after a brief pause, Stanley strained to respond: "Oh, good to see you…"

His voice was weak and unsteady, and the look in his eyes told me something wasn't right. The men helping him to stand and walk informed me that they were his younger brother and a friend. They shared that Stanley was leaving to stay with them in the country for a while.

Sensing that I should move along and get out of their way, I told Stanley how amazing it was to see him before excusing myself and heading towards the front entrance.

My head spun as I walked around the corner and processed what I'd just seen. What the hell was going on with Stanley? Did he have a stroke? Was he dying? Whatever was happening, it didn't look good.

It hadn't felt right to interrupt him and his companions further and ask questions, but now my mind exploded with possibilities and concerns. Was that the last time I would ever see Stanley? I entered my building and wished I could have more clarity on what was happening.

After climbing the stairs to my floor, I noticed a woman down the hall stepping out from Stanley's apartment and realized that this was my chance. After approaching her and saying hello, I shared that I was a friend of Stanley's and was curious what was happening with him.

She told me she was Stanley's niece and that he had suffered a suspected blood clot (which explained his weakened state). Despite this medical emergency, Stanley had insisted that he remain home alone. But his

Five

family (including her) felt he needed assistance and support as he navigated a serious (and potentially life-threatening) challenge. So, they were taking him to get proper care and then to stay with them.

"You know he's ninety-two years old," she said. "We've all been so worried about him. And as much as he wants to be here and live independently, I don't think that will be possible anymore. At his age, these kinds of health setbacks can really change everything. I honestly don't think it's likely that he'll come back here again."

After speaking for a few minutes, I thanked Stanley's niece for graciously sharing this information and wished her the best. I stumbled back to my apartment in a daze. Given everything I'd just been told, I wasn't sure I would ever get to see Stanley again. As I paced around and let that possibility sink in, I felt a wave of sadness and rage. I wanted to punch a hole in the wall I was so angry. I wanted to scream at the stupidity of a world where beautiful people disappear.

Over the following days, as this harsh new reality settled in, my rage subsided, and I was overcome by regret. I wished I'd somehow said more - that I had expressed my appreciation for this man more clearly. Unsure of what the future held, I berated myself for not having communicated more love and gratitude to this special neighbour of mine.

When I walked through the lobby of our building and made regular trips to the grocery store, I felt Stanley's absence like a gaping hole in my world. One of the best things was gone. A bright light wasn't in the place it was supposed to be. It wasn't shining where it was supposed to shine. And though I couldn't shake the sense of regret that I had somehow held back or missed an opportunity while that person was around - I could also see how this wasn't entirely true. I remembered that there had been countless times when I communicated in plain and direct language how much I admired Stanley - compelled to do so by some unseen force. After messing up and holding my feelings back so many times in the past (and living with the pain of that regret), I did not dare make the same mistake again. I pushed myself to speak from my heart.

Still, I couldn't shake the regret - a feeling that I'd somehow failed to express all the love I could have. And I wondered if that was because, as much as we may try to share love here on Earth, it's never really enough. Nothing could ever communicate it fully. There always could have been more - because that's how big love is. It's infinite. It could never feel complete. It could never be enough.

A few weeks after Stanley left, I ran into my neighbour Ron on the street. To my relief, he had an update regarding Stanley's situation. Ron shared that our elder neighbour had suffered a blood clot and was staying in a hospital several hours north of the city, near the town where his brother lived.

Ron had been speaking to Stanley on the phone every other day and expressed his concern that we

Five

might not see our beloved neighbour back home again. Ron also informed me that he'd taken the initiative to collect Christmas cards for Stanley from any of our neighbours who would like to send one - and invited me to drop off a card at his apartment over the next several days. He planned to collect these cards and send them off as soon as possible so they would have plenty of time to travel by post and arrive for Stanley before Christmas.

After sharing his plan, Ron added: "It's truly amazing how many people Stanley knows and has befriended over the years. He's always playing bridge with one friend, going for dinner with another, or being visited by somebody. He's ninety-two years old, and his social life is far more active than mine and most people I know! I think that's his secret - it's why he's lasted so long. He's the definition of alone but not lonely."

I agreed. It was remarkable.

The following day, I bought a simple Christmas card. I wrote a heartfelt message to Stanley in it, telling him how his presence was sorely missed, that I looked forward to seeing him back in our neighbourhood, and was sending positive energy his way. I was grateful to Ron for taking the initiative to organize this, and the next time I ran into him on the street, I let him know how much it meant.

During this interaction, Ron told me that he was heading south for the winter later that week, so we exchanged phone numbers - and he assured me that he'd let me know if there were any further updates regarding Stanley.

A different kind of power

Before we said goodbye, I asked Ron if he'd spoken to our elder neighbour recently or heard how he was doing. A pained look came across Ron's face that said more than any of his words. He described several newly discovered medical issues Stanley had been diagnosed with, using big words that I didn't understand. The overall sentiment was that our friend was facing some significant health challenges - and at his age, that could mean requiring assistance with living from now on.

Ron confessed that while he knew Stanley wanted nothing more than to be back home, he wasn't sure if that would ever be possible again.

"Well," I replied, "I guess anything is possible!" On that note, we shook hands and wished each other a Merry Christmas before going our separate ways.

Months passed without any word from Ron, and I wondered what happened to Stanley. I still felt his absence every day - as though something vital had been removed from the place I called home - and I thought of him fondly. Then, one morning, I came home from my walk to find a note slid underneath my apartment door. It was a small piece of paper with a handwritten message scrawled on it by the woman who lived two doors down from me, Jane.

Jane wrote that she'd received a phone call from Ron, who broke the news that Stanley was back home, to her astonishment and disbelief. Ron had told her to deliver

Five

this news to me. At the bottom of the message, Jane left her phone number and invited me to call if I wanted to ask any questions.

I couldn't believe my eyes - it seemed like a miracle. None of us thought we'd ever see Stanley again, and he was suddenly back. I grabbed my phone and called my neighbour to find out more.

When Jane answered, I thanked her for the note sharing this wonderful news. She explained that she was just as shocked as I was by this development - and knew little more than what was written on the note she'd slid beneath my door. Jane assumed that Stanley was still convalescing. And, to avoid disturbing him unnecessarily, she had simply left a note on his door, letting him know that she would be happy to help him with anything he needed. At the end of our conversation, we agreed to update each other when we found out more, and I thanked Jane again for delivering this news and taking my call before saying goodbye.

Several weeks later, I was walking to work on a dark, rainy winter night when I saw something far off in the distance that I recognized. In the misty, dim light, the vague silhouette of a human figure appeared, walking slowly toward me, and my heart jumped. Though I could barely see this shadowy form, I thought it might be Stanley.

As I approached that distant, dark blur, my hunch proved correct. Stanley was strolling along the rainy sidewalk, assisted by a rolling walker he was leaning on and two people - one on each side of him - as he moved at a gradual pace.

A different kind of power

Incapable of containing my excitement, I blurted out: "Stanley! It's amazing to see you - what an absolute pleasure to find you out here!"

It was immediately apparent that Stanley's energy was strained as he walked. After a moment of recognition, he offered a warm hello and introduced me to the family members accompanying him.

Not wishing to interfere or add any more stress to Stanley's outing, I quickly reiterated my excitement to cross paths with him and carried on my way, astonished. There was something surreal about that scene - the drizzling rain reflecting the dull amber glow of the streetlamp-illuminated night - and Stanley appearing out of the mist, flanked by two smiling, quiet helpers. He was back, he was alive, and it really did feel like a miracle.

It was some time before I saw Stanley again. When I finally did, he was sitting on a chair in the front lobby of our building, and I stopped, took a seat across from him, and chatted for a while. He shared that his energy was quite a bit lower than before, but overall, he was thrilled to be back home and getting by just fine.

"I have no complaints," he said, regardless of the long list of things he could have complained about.

I told him I would be more than happy to lend a helping hand in any way he needed, which he acknowledged and was thankful for - though he said he

Five

didn't need assistance with anything. By now, I'd learned that Stanley was a fiercely independent soul - a quality so strong in him that I had to wonder if it contributed to his longevity - if it was part of why he was still here. Where others might have folded and given up long ago, Stanley maintained a remarkably vibrant, fighting spirit. It was impressive to behold, and I knew I could learn some things from it.

Over the following weeks and months, I slowly began to see Stanley out and about more often. As the weather warmed up, his energy and health seemed to improve, and it was a pleasure to cross paths with him regularly. Now, Stanley moved around with the assistance of a rolling walker instead of his old cane. This piece of equipment conveniently doubled as a chair, which he frequently paused to sit on while making his way to the grocery store or to grab a coffee. I was able, once again, to stop and chat with him when we saw each other, always making sure he knew that I was happy to help if he needed anything.

During this time, I began to visit Stanley at his apartment occasionally, and I think we were both grateful for the company and conversations. One afternoon, he invited me over for a glass of wine, and we spoke for several hours in the comfort of his living room. Stanley shared stories from his long and fascinating life and asked me what was happening in mine.

"Have you found a nice young woman to start seeing, Miles?" he asked.

A different kind of power

I laughed and answered: "Well, I do have an update on that front, Stanley."

"Oh, great!" he replied.

"You might not like it, but it is an update. I still haven't been with anyone whatsoever. There's nothing even on my radar. But I feel happy. I wonder if I'm doing something wrong or hiding from love and intimacy almost every day. But at the same time, I honestly feel like I've been listening to myself, and nothing right has shown up yet."

"Well," he said, "that's the most important thing. You have to listen to what feels right for you. That's all that matters."

He delivered those words with a directness and intensity that struck me.

As our conversation flowed over the following hours, I periodically topped up our glasses with wine. That evening, I learned many new things about my neighbour. At one point, I asked him a broad question: "What do you think the most important thing in life is, Stanley?"

He paused, leaned back in his chair, and reflected. "That's a good question," he said, taking his time to patiently consider it before answering.

"Well, family is very important. I think you've learned that."

I nodded my head.

"And, you need to learn to like yourself. You have to be very open-minded about who you are and who you might be. Life is much easier if you are happy with yourself and like your own company. I've always been

Five

lucky that way - I'm quite content to sit here alone for a day or more. I really am. It's a wonderful thing to be happy with yourself. And, if you can't stand to be with yourself, you're in trouble."

Stanley paused to think before continuing: "And friendship. Friendship is very important. I've been fortunate to have many wonderful friends throughout my life. Very fortunate. And you know, I'm extremely grateful for my friendship with you, Miles. It's really been such a pleasure getting to know you, and I am thrilled to have you as a friend."

As Stanley spoke, he looked at me with a directness and sincerity that was moving. He shared more kind words of appreciation, and I echoed his sentiment. I felt incredibly grateful for the presence of this gracious, wise elder in my world - in a way that I suspected he could not understand. Yet, at that moment, his warmth and gratitude for our friendship caught me off guard. He seemed genuinely as excited as I was to have this unique, special person in his world, and I was touched by that. It's a strange and wonderful thing when someone likes you in a way that reflects how you feel about them.

In the days following that conversation, I thought about the questions I had asked Stanley and the simple wisdom of his answers. Friendship is one of the purest forms of spiritual wealth and one of the most beautiful things in this life. And I was deeply grateful for this friend, who held something different from everyone else in my world - a perspective far beyond my own. When I felt like complaining about the petty dramas of my comfortable and privileged life, I could remember my friend Stanley, take a deep breath, and come back to a bigger perspective. The truth was, I had been blessed with another day on this Earth. I rarely had anything to complain about. But I could so easily get caught up meditating on what I was not, who I had not become, the things I had not achieved, and the love I had not found. And yet here, at this moment, I was already rich. I had a beating heart, a place to call home, the Earth to walk on, and the people I loved. In a world of distractions, I needed to remind myself that, like my friend Stanley, I was already rich.

Six

It was a busy Saturday night in the restaurant when I greeted a family of five sitting together at a table. The mother and father of this group looked a bit younger than my parents, and their three children appeared to be in their early to mid-twenties. After introducing myself, I asked if they were celebrating anything in particular, and the mother answered awkwardly: "Oh, kind of... well, not really."

Sensing a tenderness behind her words, I decided to brush past that question and respect whatever private or vulnerable matter I might be intruding upon. Over the next two hours, this group revealed themselves to be very kind, funny, and warm. The mother and father were particularly open with me, teasing me and cracking jokes as I served them. When they were done eating dinner, the children abruptly departed for the evening, leaving their parents alone with a bottle of wine to finish together. As the two of them sat and relaxed, I asked if they needed anything, letting them know that there was no rush and they should take as long as they liked to enjoy themselves. I could see how happy they were.

"We're perfect right now, Miles," the mother said. "This has been such a beautiful night. Thank you so much."

Rushing off to greet another table of guests, I felt the sincerity of that couple's gratitude to simply be together at that moment.

The next time I did my rounds and checked to see if they had everything they needed, I decided to ask them one of my favourite questions to pose to people I was serving. Typically, I reserved this question for married couples celebrating a significant anniversary after decades together. On such occasions, I would ask: "You two have managed to stay together all this time - what have you learned? What's the secret to a lasting relationship? What wisdom can you share with me?"

Although this couple was not celebrating an anniversary, their warmth and affection made me want to ask them that question regardless. So, I inquired: "How long have you two been married?"

The wife immediately replied with a tone of shock and indignation: "You can't ask old people that question!"

Unsure if she was joking or sincerely offended, I held my ground and said: "Oh, well - I just assumed you two have been together for a while, given the three kids you were with tonight. And I love learning about how people make a relationship work over time. It's a rare thing, you know, for people to stay together. And I'm

Six

always curious to understand how couples have accomplished that."

As I spoke, the woman began to smile and laugh, and I was relieved that she hadn't been offended by my question and was just giving me a hard time.

"We've been together for twenty-three years," the husband said, reaching over to place his hand on top of his wife's in a gesture of affection.

"That's amazing!" I replied. "How have you done it? What have you learned - what's the secret to a successful marriage?"

"There's no secret," the man said, lounging back in his chair, laughing and sighing. "And I'm an emotional mess most of the time. There's no secret. It's hard. Life has ups and downs. You just gotta ride it. And I'm a basket case."

As I listened, I felt like I was hearing two answers to my question: One that this man was giving on the surface and another that was right beneath his words. The humility of his response was remarkable, and it would be a powerful gift to bring to any relationship.

Then, his wife interrupted: "This man has the most beautiful heart in the entire world! I am so blessed to know him and have him in my life."

She continued to gush over her husband for some time, showering him with words of praise and gratitude. Given the sincerity of his response to my question, I believed her. Then, she looked at me and said: "Nobody has ever asked us a question like that. That is such a profound question. You're not a normal person, Miles. There's something special about you…"

A different kind of power

ted her kind words, but she continued, ⎯aight into my eyes as she spoke: "Okay, Miles. ⎯re's something I need to tell you. This might seem really weird, but I think I have to share this." She paused, took a breath, and said: "I think you're here for a reason tonight. I'm going to be honest - this has been one of the most painful and beautiful days of my life. My father - he's been fighting cancer for months, and this morning he passed away..."

"I'm so sorry," I said.

"Thank you. I appreciate that. It's been such a wild day. We were just talking about it - I don't even have words to describe what's happening. And you might think I'm crazy, but everything today has felt like a miracle. I can feel Dad with us - he has been helping us with everything all day. Everything that has happened has been so beautiful and perfect - like we're being guided or held by him. It's one of the hardest days of my life, and this might sound crazy to you, but something really magical is happening, and you're a part of it."

As she spoke, she broke into tears.

I nodded and said: "I understand. None of that sounds crazy to me."

Speaking through tears, she continued: "The way you've been this whole night and the fact that you asked that question - it's just so profound! You helped us reflect on how lucky we are to have each other. It's so beautiful, Miles. You're a very special person..."

She reached across the table toward me and said: "Can I hold your hands for a minute? I just want you to

Six

know how much your presence here means. I want to share this energy with you - you're part of it."

Without hesitating, I reached my hands out to hers, tears streaming down my face. And for the next several minutes, she continued sharing from her heart as we held hands. For that time, we weren't strangers in a busy, fancy restaurant on a Saturday night. The world around us faded away, and we were there as souls, connecting in a moment of grief, love, and gratitude.

Eventually, the moment was over, and I returned to the reality of being a server in a restaurant with half a dozen other tables impatiently waiting for me. I told this lovely couple I would be back with their bill shortly and raced off to take another group's order.

When I returned a few minutes later, they expressed their gratitude once again for my presence that evening, and we exchanged tender hugs before they disappeared into the night.

Drying my face, I walked into the back of the restaurant and told one of my coworkers: "I just cried my eyes out and held hands with a woman at one of my tables."

"You did what, Miles?" she replied, and I described the encounter that just took place.

"Oh my god, that's so beautiful!" she exclaimed. "I've gotta start using that question with my tables."

We laughed, and I stumbled through the restaurant in awe for the rest of the night. That lovely couple had reacted as though I had done something special or heroic with them, but all I did was ask a simple question and listen.

A different kind of power

Over the years of working at that restaurant, my job became less an experience in drudgery and more an opportunity to immerse myself in sacred human connection. There were shifts when my mood was so joyful and ebullient that my coworkers rolled their eyes in cynical confusion, wishing they were anywhere else and wondering what drug I was on. Maybe it was the years of loneliness and sadness I'd endured - or perhaps it was the loneliness and sadness of life at that moment - but what seemed to be a hopelessly mundane workplace to some of my peers was something I often cherished as a necessary medicine for my heart. During many evenings at work, there was nowhere else that I would have rather been. It didn't bother me when coworkers complained about the job as though it were a hopeless, dead-end trap. I understood that for some of them, that was true. They were going through things that were very different from me. And, occasionally, I felt just as cynical - my faith in humanity injured by one too many cruel customers.

Many of the people I worked with also loved their jobs and cherished their time in that place. And some days, I was the grumpiest, moodiest one in the building. I suppose we all took our turns in that role. But, for the most part, I didn't take my time there for granted. For every moment that I was moody, frustrated, or entitled,

Six

I tried to be kind, supportive, or helpful several times over. I considered myself lucky to just be there.

One Saturday night, after a long and tiring shift, I got home to my empty apartment, ready to collapse into a quiet, restful evening, when I noticed a pain at the back of my throat. I'd been feeling this pain for the previous two weeks - a ball of tension that, for lack of better words, felt like the physical manifestation of a dull, aching sadness.

During quiet moments alone, it was more noticeable. But even amid the busyness, stress, and laughter of my workplace, it was always there in the background - a pain I carried in my throat that simply wouldn't go away. And it felt distinctly sad. It was a strange thing - and it made me realize how peaceful and happy the past season of my life had been. I was no longer used to feeling sad all the time. In fact, I had gotten so used to feeling grateful and happy I didn't quite know what to do with this sadness. And now, as I wound down for the night, I was disturbed that the feeling was getting stronger. It was no longer a subtlety that I could notice and ignore. It was intense and felt like it was screaming for attention.

So, as I sat alone in my apartment, instead of staring at the screen of my phone or otherwise distracting myself, I decided to pull out some blank paper, find a pen, and write.

A different kind of power

Given how strong and confusing this feeling was, I wondered if scribbling my emotions out onto an empty page might be helpful. Once I located my supplies, I sat down at my desk. I began to write spontaneously - trying to bypass any filters or barriers to direct, raw expression.

After a minute of scribbling simple, stream-of-consciousness words and statements (such as *I'm sad. I feel sad. There's sadness in me...*), a distinct voice emerged. It was the voice of what might be best described as my five-year-old self. As I continued pouring a stream of unfiltered words and feelings onto the page, I wrote from this young, innocent voice: *"I'm sad. I just want to play - I just want to do something fun. We never get to do something fun."*

Sitting hunched over my desk, everything suddenly made sense. This ball of sadness in my throat - it was my inner child who just wanted to have some fun and feel loved. Over the previous several months, I had been doing a decent job of organizing my life as an adult. I'd been working at the restaurant more than usual and focusing my efforts on effectively marketing my writing (and seeing success in that area for the first time). But this little guy - the innocent kid in me who loved life deeply - felt like he'd been left out in the cold. Life was all serious and grown up. He never got to do anything fun.

I continued writing for a while, letting this tender voice speak freely into my messy, rapid handwriting, and a pure yearning for love and life came clearly into view. Eventually, I leaned back into my chair and

Six

realized I needed to do something. Instead of passively listening to this aching part of me and letting him wallow in sadness, I had to take action.

So, I told him we would do something special just for him - we would have some fun and enjoy ourselves. I had the following night off from work, so we could do whatever he wanted - it would be a special evening just for him. Then, I asked my inner five-year-old what he wanted to do.

As I sat and listened with curiosity, an answer became clear almost immediately: He wanted to go to the movies - to see a film at the theatre.

Considering that I'd just given this part of me the opportunity to choose anything he wanted, going to see a movie seemed like a rather humble possibility. But, at the same time, watching a film at the cinema was something I had not done in years. And while it wasn't what I might have guessed would be at the top of a bucket list for my inner child, something about it felt perfect. For a kid, it made sense.

Once it was settled that this would be the special activity, I checked the current movie listings at nearby theatres to see what film my inner five-year-old was most excited about. The list of features included the new *Ghostbusters* movie, *Planet Of The Apes*, *Godzilla vs King Kong*, and several other action films and dramas. I thought *Ghostbusters* would be the natural choice, but my inner child had a different idea: He was only interested in *Godzilla vs King Kong*.

My adult mind was horrified by this. Under normal circumstances, I would never have considered watching

A different kind of power

that film - much less going to a theatre to do so publicly. I tried to reason and rationalize that this must be some kind of mistake, but the child-voice in me did not budge. His decision had already been made. So far as he was concerned, anything else would be a complete disappointment. So, I shrugged my shoulders and accepted that he'd made up his mind. We were going to *Godzilla vs King Kong*.

The following evening, I left my apartment to walk towards the theatre with plenty of time to spare before the movie's showtime. I decided to make this a dinner date and grab something to eat before catching the film. As I walked toward the busyness of downtown, I told my inner child that we could eat anywhere he wanted. I assumed that he might have expensive taste and was prepared for that. This was a special occasion - nothing was off-limits. But when a man walked past us holding a pizza box, the decision was made instantly. The child in me wanted pizza.

Surprised by the simplicity of this choice, I figured I would wait to see if something more sophisticated or fancy was appealing once we started to walk past restaurants. Then, another man carrying a pizza box in his hands walked by, and it was over. The five-year-old voice in me took this as a sign that pizza was mandatory. There was nothing else that made any sense whatsoever.

As I accepted this decision, I told my inner child that we could get pizza anywhere - there were no limits. I envisioned us sitting down for a nice, gourmet, thin-crust pizza dinner. It was immediately apparent,

Six

however, that this part of me was only interested in the cheapest, sloppiest pizza available. He wanted some big, delicious slices of the most basic, greasy pizza there was. My adult mind was again confused, wondering why this part of me wanted something so crass and uncultured. But the answer was obvious: He was a kid. He didn't want dumb, grown-up stuff.

So, I shrugged my shoulders, and instead of going to a nice restaurant to sit down for a special meal, I did something much more out of the ordinary: I went to a tiny, dingy, cheap pizza slice place. I ordered a couple of big, sloppy slices served on a thin paper plate and sat alone in a dark, desolate corner of the cramped establishment with a bizarre sense of joy. I rarely ate pizza and would never have come and sat in this undecorated, cold industrial place. And, maybe because this was all out of character for me, there was something surprisingly uncomfortable and vulnerable about it. For my inner five-year-old, that seemed to make it all the more satisfying. As my ego squirmed, he was overflowing with happiness.

After I finished my pizza (which was admittedly delicious), it was time to head to the theatre, just a short walk away. When I arrived outside of it, I started to have second thoughts. Was I really about to go watch a *King Kong* movie alone? A shame-filled voice rang through my head, assuring me that this was a terrible, embarrassing idea and that I should just call it a night and walk home. But I took a breath and remembered that however absurd this might be, I'd made a promise and couldn't break it now. So, with a strange feeling of

A different kind of power

vulnerability, I entered the theatre, purchased a ticket, got a large popcorn and found my seat.

After watching a marathon of advertisements and previews, the movie began. And for reasons I still don't fully comprehend, I began to cry. Throughout that film, I cried so many times I lost track. Part of this was a reaction to the movie itself - which, it turned out, was a phenomenal pick by my inner child. Another part of it might have simply been that I was there, doing this for him. Everything about that moment - the oversalted popcorn, the hushed excitement of the dark cinema, the amazing fantasy-action scenes, and the deep symbolic meaning behind everything in that film - unlocked a steady stream of tears. Again, I can't pretend to understand why, but something about it all was deeply meaningful. As I cried, it felt healing.

When the film was over, I walked home through the city streets with a heart overflowing - beaming with love and gratitude at the beauty of monsters, movies, pizza, popcorn, and being alive. I felt incredible.

The most interesting part of this experience was what happened following it: The feeling of sadness in my throat that had haunted me for weeks was gone. The sense of being neglected was no longer there, and in its wake was a feeling of inner richness, light, and gratitude for the wonderful people and things in my life. After doing something so small and simple to love and support a young, innocent part of me, I was much less reactive and moody in my daily existence. I felt more generous, buoyant, and strong. It was almost like I'd charged something in me - I'd filled a place with

Six

love, so now I had more love to give. It was significant - and made me appreciate how powerful such a simple act of nurturance can be.

After that first movie night, I began habitually taking my inner child out to the cinema about once a month. It was such an enjoyable and impactful experience that it only made sense to do it regularly.

The second film I went to see was a children's movie called *IF*. Once again, this was not a film my adult mind would have ever entertained watching or going to see in person - it was a kid's movie about imaginary friends (which is what the title of the film, *IF*, was an acronym for). To my inner child, however, this was absolutely perfect. And it wasn't lost on me that, in a sense, this whole endeavour was a manifestation of my relationship with what could be considered an imaginary friend.

On the evening when I decided to go see *IF*, I was walking to the theatre when I was suddenly struck by a thought that I had innocently failed to consider: It might not be socially acceptable or appropriate for a grown man to go watch a children's movie alone in a theatre. In fact, it might be seen as weird or even creepy behaviour. As I pondered the heaviness of this perspective, I realized that I probably couldn't go through with this. It was too much - too weird.

Unsure of myself, I texted a friend to ask for their thoughts on this matter but received no immediate response. Desperate for some kind of outside perspective, I turned to google as I continued walking slowly toward the cinema, asking the question: *Is it okay*

A different kind of power

for a grown man to go and watch a children's movie alone in a theatre?

There were several forums where people had asked and answered this question. Almost every response to it was supportive and kind. Many adults spoke with pride about going to see a variety of children's films alone. Still, I wasn't sure - and didn't think I could do it.

When I arrived at the theatre, I sat down on a ledge by the front doors, torn by this conflict.

The shame and embarrassment seemed too severe, and I decided to turn around and walk home. I knew how much my inner child wanted to see that movie, but going alone was too weird.

But then, just before abandoning this mission, I remembered the purity of my intentions. I remembered what I was doing: Bringing my inner five-year-old out for a wholesome good time. And I asked myself if that was actually something to be ashamed of? I knew it was not.

I continued to challenge myself: "Are you going to let the possibility of looking weird stop you from doing something beautiful? Is that how you want to live your life?"

Again, the answer was no. So, I took a deep breath, walked through the theatre doors, bought one ticket to the children's movie about imaginary friends, got some popcorn, and walked to my seat. I felt a sting of awkwardness as I sat down, but I knew there was no turning back.

A handful of couples slowly trickled into the theatre after me, and I realized that, given the neighbourhood

Six

this theatre was in and the time of the screening, there might not even be any children present. Only one family with kids showed up before the lights dimmed and trailers began. I relaxed into my seat, realizing there was nothing weird or noticeable about my being there.

The moment the film began, I started to cry. And to be honest, I cried off and on throughout the duration of the movie. Something about the storyline, the imagery, and the perfection of being there that evening touched a deep part of me. There were moments when I had to restrain myself from sobbing loudly. When the movie ended, I dried my cheeks and realized, once again, that my inner child had excellent taste. Walking home, I felt charged, nourished, and revitalized.

The following morning, I woke up to a message from a former manager at the restaurant, David. It had been a couple of years since David left my workplace for a position at another restaurant, and I often thought of him fondly. We worked together for a year or so, and over that time, it seemed as though every soul employed under that roof fell in love with David. He was such a kind, thoughtful, and warm person that his presence transformed our little corner of the world. It was a sad day when he departed from our restaurant and said goodbye.

While working alongside one another, David occasionally listened to my podcast and came to work eager to discuss the latest episode. He was always sincere, curious, and supportive during these conversations, and I appreciated his open-minded, unique perspective.

When I saw that David had sent a message this particular morning, I was delighted to hear from him and opened it with excitement. It read: "You're not going to believe this, Miles, but I experienced the exact same thing that you did when I was five years old. I lost my wallet, just like you. Almost every detail of our stories is the same. I was on a trip with my family. I put my wallet down somewhere and forgot it, and it was heartbreaking. The memory is still so clear. Pretty wild!"

As I read these words, I knew exactly what David was talking about - and was stunned by our eerily common experiences. He was referencing a childhood story I shared in my most recent podcast (and that I had written about in the past) - a story he clearly had his own parallel version of.

For the sake of clarity, I will briefly recount this experience here: When I was five years old, I went on a trip to the city with my family. It was my Grandpa's seventieth birthday, and relatives from all over were congregating for a big, chaotic celebration. My parents, brothers, and I were staying with my Aunt and Uncle at their fancy new house - and I had big plans for this trip. I'd brought my little wallet with me to the city, a wallet where I'd been stashing all of the money I'd saved up to that point in my brief life. My intention was to visit the cool malls and shops of the city, where I could find exciting things to buy with my small fortune. I don't

Six

remember the exact amount of money I had saved in that little wallet, but it was around fifty dollars - a significant sum for my five-year-old self.

On the first morning of our stay, tragedy struck: When I went to get my wallet, I couldn't find it. In a state of panic, I looked everywhere for it, asking everyone in the house if they'd seen it. Nobody had. Eventually, after my search proved futile, I faced the devastating reality: My wallet - and the entire fortune I saved inside it - was gone. And I was left to face the crushing sadness of this loss. That was that. Life went on.

But this is not where the story ends. Almost three decades later, I was meditating one afternoon when a sad, childlike voice came into my awareness. This sad voice felt distinctly like my five-year-old self. And when I asked this young part of me why he was so down, he explained that he'd lost his wallet. In an instant, I knew exactly what he was talking about. The memory of that weekend in the city all those years ago came rushing back to me as though it had just happened. Given how sad this young part of me felt, it seemed like that loss was still just as fresh and alive in him as it had been on the day when it happened. Sitting in silence, I tried my best to be kind and understanding to this young part of me. I felt his feelings and tried to validate them. And that was that. The meditation ended, and I got up and continued my day.

The next time I sat down to meditate, he was there again - still sad about his lost wallet. Again, I listened to him and did my best to offer understanding and support. When the meditation was over, I returned to my day - but he wouldn't go away.

I began to feel his presence every time I meditated. And his sadness did not become any less intense. Though I continued to be open, curious, and understanding when I felt his presence, he continued in his despair.

One afternoon during a meditation, as I felt the desolation and disappointment of this young part of me again, I realized how foolish I had been. This kid was waiting for someone to do something that would make what had happened all those years ago right. He'd been waiting for someone to do something to help him for decades. And here I was, totally capable of being that person for him. He was waiting and longing for something I could do easily - but I'd just been sitting idly and letting him wallow in sadness.

In that instant, I shot up from my meditation, put on a sweater and a pair of shoes, went outside, grabbed my bicycle, and headed towards the nearest mall. It was time to get a new wallet for this little guy.

When I got to the mall, I walked into a store that I knew had a variety of wallets and went to look at them. I kept the voice of that five-year-old kid alive in my awareness, treating this whole shopping trip as a kind of active meditation. I asked him which of the wallets there he liked most - which one was coolest. He selected a small, minimalist wallet that he felt was particularly slick, and that was the one. I took it to the cashier, bought it, and proceeded to the nearest ATM. There, I withdrew fifty dollars (nearly all of my money at that

Six

particular moment) and placed it ceremoniously into the brand-new wallet. The lost fortune and lost wallet had been restored. And the kid in me who had been so sad and deflated suddenly felt like the whole world was a beautiful, loving, hope-filled place.

For several months following that trip to the mall with my inner child, I felt an unusual sense of optimism, gratitude, and happiness. The sad voice that had been haunting my quiet moments was transformed into something altogether different - the deflated kid was now exuberant. The effects of that little trip to the mall reverberated through my life and my relationship with the world.

Now, after many years had passed (and the wallet I bought that day at the mall had nearly disintegrated from wear and tear), I read David's message with a sense of wonder and understanding. He'd heard my story, and it was remarkable that something so similar happened to both of us at the same age on a family trip. We were both five years old. We'd put all our money into our wallets. And then they were gone. After digesting his words, I went for my morning walk and contemplated how to respond to such a profound revelation. Then, I suddenly felt a familiar presence come alive in me. It was my five-year-old self, and he had an idea: We needed to replace David's lost fortune.

My inner child felt a sense of urgency - this opportunity was too good to pass up. David was one of the most beautiful people I'd ever met, and his story was exactly what I'd been through. As far as my inner child was concerned, there was only one possible response.

Initially, I planned to send David an electronic money transfer to replace his childhood loss. But to send this quietly via my bank, I needed David's email address. So, I messaged another one of my managers (who I knew was friends with David) to secretly ask for this information. By the time I got a response, however, my inner child had made it clear that sending an electronic money transfer would not be sufficient. This innocent voice in me was certain that for David's inner child to really receive this gift, it had to be physical. David had to be able to touch it and hold it for it to be real. So, given that it was my day off and I didn't have much of a choice in this matter, I accepted that I had a clear mission: Go find the perfect wallet for David, put the lost money back into it, and then quietly deliver it to his workplace.

I knew that the more time I gave myself to think about this plan, the greater the risk that my mind would jump in and ruin everything by finding reasons to hesitate and rationalize my way out of such a strange and vulnerable act. So, before that could happen, I ate a quick snack and headed downtown to fulfill this dream.

When I arrived at the busy retail district, I went to a department store with a large selection of wallets and carefully searched for the perfect one. As I browsed, I listened to the child voice in me for guidance, hoping he would point out the right wallet and lead the way. There were *Spider-Man* wallets, *Friends*-themed wallets, and a

Six

variety of more elegant and stoic adult options. When I picked up one wallet with the word *roots* embossed on its leather surface, the child voice in me exclaimed: *"It's perfect! This is all about David's roots. It's perfect!"*

So, I trusted my gut and took that wallet to the checkout. On my way, I stopped to grab a small gift bag to place the wallet into, selecting a simple, nondescript bag that seemed perfect to conceal the surprise I would hide inside it. After paying at the till, I walked out onto a busy downtown street and made my way to catch a bus toward David's work. When I stopped for a moment to put the wallet into the gift bag, a woman walked past me with a t-shirt that caught my attention. A message in bold, large print was written across it that read: *Rooted In Love.*

I thought about the *roots* wallet I'd just selected and felt like this was some kind of divine confirmation that I had, in fact, made the correct choice. *"It's perfect,"* the child voice in me said, and I placed a single one-hundred dollar bill into the wallet before putting it into the gift bag. I had no idea how much money David lost all those years ago, but I assumed it was similar to the amount I had lost, and one hundred dollars seemed like the perfect replacement.

It took me about an hour on public transit to get to the restaurant where David worked as a manager. By the time I neared my destination, I began to wonder if what I was doing was absolutely ridiculous and insane. But I'd come too far and invested too much into this plan to abandon it now - so I carried on.

A different kind of power

When I got off the bus within a block of the restaurant, I walked to a grassy field where I paused to collect myself. After finding a fallen log to sit down on, I wondered what to write on the tiny card attached to the handle of the gift bag I was holding. After a moment of reflection, I wrote:

"To Mister David Thomas - from a kid who can relate."

With the gift now complete, I walked to the restaurant and, as I approached the front door, turned around - overcome by fear. I couldn't bring myself to do it, so I decided to take a lap around the block and reconsider.

"This is insane," I thought to myself. "This is the corniest thing ever." For a moment, the voices of shame and insecurity begged me to stop and cancel this mission, assuring me that nothing good could possibly come from it. But, instead of bowing down before their convincing rhetoric, I took a deep breath and reflected on the reality of what I was about to do. I reflected on how special of a person David was and how beautiful it felt to do something to show my appreciation for him. I thought about choosing a life of shameless love instead of hiding and living in fear. Tears came to my eyes, and I knew what I had to do. I collected myself, headed back toward the restaurant's entrance, and this time I walked in.

I was greeted by a couple of kind young hosts at the front desk and asked them if David was working. They replied that they hadn't seen him and didn't think he was around. Then, before our conversation could go any

Six

further, another manager approached and asked if she could help. I repeated my question to her, and she shared that David had already gone home for the afternoon.

Without thinking, I said: "Perfect - I have a gift for him. Could you make sure that he gets it?"

I handed her the small gift bag, and she smiled and said: "Of course!"

After thanking her, I strolled out of the restaurant, giddy with excitement. The mission had been accomplished. And no matter how it was received, the adventure of going through with it had been amazing.

Several days passed after my journey to David's workplace, and I heard nothing from him. I knew he was a busy man - a husband with young children and a manager with plenty of responsibilities on his shoulders. He might not have received the gift yet - or he could have been too busy to write to me about it.

More days passed, and I heard nothing. I wondered if the gift had even reached David - or if he had received it but didn't know who it came from (given the cryptic message I wrote on it). None of this was too worrying—after all, listening to my heart and doing something sincere for a good person had already enriched my world. Still, as the days passed, my curiosity grew.

After a week, I wondered if I should reach out to David and covertly ask if he'd gotten the wallet without revealing too much. My only worry was that he might not have received it. If that was the case, I was fully prepared to get him another wallet and repeat this act immediately.

But before I could give this too much thought, I got a message from David.

In it, he shared that he'd been trying to figure out what to say for the past week. He explained that this had been such a touching gesture he was at a loss for words - that receiving the wallet had been a very special moment. After writing some incredibly kind things, he ended his message by signing it: *"From the kid with the coolest wallet."*

My eyes filled with tears, and for that moment, everything about life felt perfect and beautiful. I was relieved to know that David had received the gift. And, given how his message was signed, the child in him had received it, too.

Seven

My Mother and I were catching up on the phone when she asked me a question I'd been wrestling with for nearly a year: "Do you have a special new woman in your life yet, Miles?"

I told her that there was nobody new, that there had been nobody new since we last spoke, and went on to explain that because I'd been so focused on other things, dating just wasn't on my radar. I responded almost defensively to her innocent question, describing the love I experienced by spending time in nature, connecting with friends, and doing creative work. I acknowledged that it was long past time for me to start dating and meeting women again, but nothing that made sense or felt right had shown up.

As I spoke, even though everything I said was technically true, I wasn't sure if I believed myself anymore. Something was slightly comical about how I nervously tripped over my words, attempting to preserve the idea that everything about my chronically solitary, single life was great.

A different kind of power

In her wisdom, my mother had little to say in response, simply replying: "Well, you'll know when the time is right."

After we got off the phone, I questioned myself. It had been years since my last relationship ended - years since I had kissed someone or held their body next to mine. Maybe I'd gotten too comfortable in isolation. Maybe something vital in me had been broken by technology and protracted solitude - a natural instinct to mate, to exchange physical touch, and to experience union in that one profound way.

And yet, I hadn't been withering inside. In a very real way, I felt more filled with love and life than I could ever remember. But this love wasn't coming from a romantic relationship or a fixation on one particular person. That part of my life had never been more empty.

This was the internal tug-of-war I'd been having for the previous year: A belief that I urgently needed to get out into the world, date, and find someone to connect with - and a complete lack of interest or motivation to put that idea into action. There was always something else that felt more enticing, immediate, and sacred - a forest to explore, a book to write, etc. And although it had been a happy, beautiful chapter of my life, I felt like I'd been failing the whole time.

This inner conflict began the previous winter when I took a large dose of psilocybin mushrooms. While under their influence, I had a powerful experience that gave me a clear message: I needed to find someone to be with. The mushrooms awakened a desire for love, intimacy, and partnership that I had long ago

Seven

disassociated from. During that trip, this desire screamed at me as though my life depended on going on dates and simply having new experiences with people. At that moment, nothing else mattered - the gravity of this need for connection hit me like a ton of bricks.

When I came out on the other side of that mushroom experience, the homework I'd been given seemed easy enough: Just go on a date. Sure, it had been a long time, and some shyness and insecurity had grown in the absence of recent experience, but how hard could it be?

Now, a whole year had passed, and I'd found countless things to do besides going on a single date. I'd been blessed with many wonderful experiences - but failed to do that simple homework assignment. The urgent voice awakened during that mushroom trip had been completely ignored - and there wasn't a week that passed when I didn't feel guilt at the back of my mind, knowing I had neglected something vital. But, I reasoned with myself, nothing had felt right. If it had, I would have pursued it. I was just following my heart. At least, that's what I told myself.

During this year, I didn't take mushrooms again. One of the reasons for this was that it felt pointless to do so before I'd accomplished the task set forth so clearly the last time I used them. I suspected that if I consumed mushrooms, the same voice would be awakened - and would inevitably punish me for my cowardice.

But now, after stubbornly ignoring that call to action for so long, I decided that I was ready for my punishment. It had been a full year of avoidance, so I felt that it might be appropriate to take a dose of psilocybin mushrooms again. Perhaps they could help me understand why it was so hard to break out of my shell and be a normal human. Maybe the harsh voice I'd been visited by last time would smack some sense into me and give me the push I needed to step out of this pattern.

It was a cold night in the dead of winter when I turned the lights down in my apartment and ceremoniously ate some of the dried psilocybin mushrooms that had been sitting in my cupboard for the previous year. After chewing a few chunks of crispy, dry, golden teacher mushrooms and washing them down with water, I put on some peaceful ambient music (selecting Jon Hopkins' album, *Music For Psychedelic Therapy*) and got comfortable.

As the gentle noise and dim lighting created a warm, serene atmosphere, I closed my eyes and began to meditate - focusing on the sensation of breathing into my heart. I felt tension and apprehension as I sat there, bracing for impact. Knowing I had failed so completely since the last time I took these mushrooms, my body contracted in preparation for the unfiltered assault of accountability that I knew was coming. With my jaw clenched and shoulders tight, I accepted that it was time to face this reckoning.

Sitting in stillness, I continued to focus on my breath and let the beautiful music soothe me. Then, something happened that caught me off guard: A wave of disorientation hit me - bending and altering my consciousness and making me slightly nauseous in the

Seven

process. After that wave passed, I took a deep breath and noticed a presence with me in the room. Suddenly, it felt like countless beings were clapping and cheering for me - like this was some kind of homecoming celebration, and I was being given a hero's welcome.

This seemed like a mistake, and I shook my head in confusion and disbelief. I was waiting to get my ass kicked by an angry, harsh voice, disappointed with my cowardice. But as I sat there, the celebratory cheering grew louder. A group of innumerable beings showered me with unconditional love, acceptance, support, and praise. This was the exact opposite of what I had been expecting.

As the celebration continued - contradicting everything I'd been preparing for - I silently asked: "Why are you celebrating? I failed. I haven't been with anyone. I didn't even go on a single date this whole year."

Then, a voice answered: "NO - YOU PASSED THE TEST! Nothing felt right to you, and you listened to yourself. YAY!!!" The voices cheered and clapped together in ecstatic celebration.

"YOU PASSED THE TEST!" they repeated. "Instead of forcing yourself to do something that didn't feel right, you stayed true to your heart. YAY!!!"

Shocked by this outpouring of support, I began to cry - feeling the love of these countless beings wash over me like a healing golden light.

The voice continued: "You followed your heart and went where love pulled you! Instead of betraying yourself and being with someone just because you thought you should - you listened! YOU PASSED THE TEST!!!"

For some time, I sat with tears streaming down my cheeks, surrounded by a symphony of joyful acceptance and praise that was the polar opposite of what I'd been waiting for. Without asking any more questions or trying to understand this plot twist more deeply, I let the energy of that procession of love fill me. It felt like arriving in heaven. And after carrying a burden of shame around this for so long, it was an incredible relief. The very thing I'd been ashamed of was being celebrated as a hero's triumphant victory.

Eventually, this celebratory moment shifted, and I found myself alone again in an instant. As I adjusted to this sudden change, I became aware of another, more subtle presence. For lack of better words, I felt the mushrooms I had just eaten - and more specifically, the consciousness or spirit of those mushrooms - studying me. With my eyes closed, I could feel what the mushrooms were feeling about me - I could hear what they were thinking as they surveyed me from the inside out.

The first thing they noticed seemed related to the Reishi mushrooms I had become familiar with over the previous year. It appeared that they regarded Reishi as extremely powerful and admirable beings - and were impressed by my close association with such a noble life form (maybe even a bit intimidated). They seemed to be in awe of the Reishi mushroom's wild, ancient, and supernatural wisdom. So, instead of being seen as the domesticated, spiritually weak, and feeble man I might

Seven

have been a year earlier (when I last took psilocybin mushrooms), I was being viewed with respect. Even the sheer amount of time I had spent in nature appeared to have done something to me that the mushrooms saw as honourable. To their eyes, something robust, wild, and healthy had grown in me.

I sat silently and observed for a while, continuing to eavesdrop on the thoughts, perceptions, and opinions of the mushrooms' consciousness. Then, everything went blank again, and I decided to lie down on the floor and focus on breathing into my heart once more.

As soon as I got settled and began taking long, deep breaths - keeping my awareness on the sensation of air travelling into, through, and around my heart - a glowing, warm feeling began to build in my chest. For a while, I lie there breathing, each inhale and exhale acting as a caress, massaging my heart open and alive. Without thinking, I raised my hands above my chest and, with my palms facing my heart, began moving them closer together, then farther apart - stretching, manipulating, and magnifying the energy that was building. As the glowing sensation grew, it became extremely joyful and barely tolerable. There was so much energy it was almost painful.

Then, like a wave breaking, the intensity dropped, and in its wake, everything felt gentle again. This heart meditation continued for some time, the music I'd been playing having long since ended. Then, as I was resting in the beautiful glow of that moment, a voice said something very clearly to me: *You don't need to take drugs to do this, Miles. Don't wait until the next time you use a*

A different kind of power

mind-altering substance to sit down and be with your heart. This should be a regular part of your life. You can do this any time you want to. Feel how important it is. Your heart is a powerful force - a source of wisdom and energy, just like the mushrooms. Come back here often.

As I lay there in the dark, I remembered how I used to meditate like this regularly. It had been quite some time since I'd done so. Feeling the glow in my chest, the message of that voice was stamped in my mind: *You don't need drugs to do this. Come back here often.*

The following night, I got home from work just after ten o'clock. I decided that instead of opening my laptop or staring at my phone and losing myself to empty distractions, I would take the advice I'd received the previous evening and meditate on my heart. After brushing my teeth and getting changed, I rolled out a mat on the floor, put on some gentle music (selecting Jon Hopkins' *Music For Psychedelic Therapy* again), laid down, and closed my eyes.

As soon as I began to focus on breathing into my heart, the feeling of glowing warmth in my chest returned, just like the previous night. With each breath in and each breath out, that glowing sensation shifted, moved, and grew - like an ember that I was blowing on, radiating more warmth with each caress of breath.

With that sensation building, I raised my hands above my chest and - palms facing toward my heart -

Seven

began using them to stretch, move, and massage the energy. It was as though I was performing some kind of improvisational, childlike energy work on myself, following an impulse with no inhibition. As I continued, the energy in my chest reached peaks that were almost uncomfortably intense, and then calmed back down. I had no idea what I was doing - aside from connecting to my heart - but it felt amazing. And that voice from the previous night had been correct: I did not need drugs to do this. Although being there with my heart almost felt like a drug.

Two weeks later, I found myself wrestling with a familiar conflict. Enough time had passed since the validation and encouragement of that mushroom trip for my mind to slip back into a well-worn path of comparison and self-doubt. Once again, I looked at my long-time singlehood with confusion and concern, wondering how I'd let myself go so long without love and if it was time to take drastic action.

I was free from this conflict when I was out in nature, being creative, or interacting with people in the real world. In such moments, I was simply happy - confident that I'd been listening to my gut and that nothing was wrong with me or my life.

Then, usually after looking at my phone or somehow comparing myself to others, I was struck by those familiar voices of doubt and shame. They told me I was

A different kind of power

a fool and a freak - that life and love were passing me by. They urged me to download a dating app and just be with someone. But I couldn't do it.

In my gut, I felt that it wasn't the right time. To be more precise, I felt like there was something particularly vulnerable or volatile about that moment in my life. It would have been incredibly easy for my heart to fall in love with a woman - especially given how long I had been starved for that kind of connection. But something told me that this was not the time to recklessly fall in love. There were other things to work on and sort out, and one impulsive choice could throw it all to pieces and have far-reaching consequences. My intuition was strangely loud and clear on this matter, but my mind was still unconvinced.

This inner conflict was all I could think about when I walked into work on a Friday afternoon, ready for a busy shift. After changing into my white dress shirt and black necktie, I headed onto the restaurant floor and waited for my first table of guests to arrive.

Then, my coworker, Angel, walked through the door.

"There you are, Big Money!" she shouted from a distance, laughing hysterically at the nickname she'd given me months earlier (and convinced most of our coworkers to embrace): *Big Money Miles.*

Holding a large, thick, hardcover book, Angel approached me and said: "I brought you a present - you're going to love this!"

Seven

"Thanks, Angel," I replied, reluctantly accepting her generous gift. "This book is huge, though - I'm not sure when I'll ever have time to read it."

"Just look at it - it's perfect for you," Angel insisted, and I suddenly got the feeling that my coworker was delivering some kind of message to me. I looked at the book's cover and read its title: INSURGENT. Then I saw the book's subtitle in bold print. It read: ONE CHOICE CAN DESTROY YOU.

My eyes widened, and I blurted out: "One choice can destroy you? Damn, Angel, that's intense!"

Angel let out a wild laugh and replied: "I told you! It's perfect for you, Big Money."

The book's ominous subtitle seemed to repeat the very warning I'd been feeling in my gut: *Be careful. Given where you're at, one choice can destroy you.*

Angel and I talked and laughed for a moment before a coworker interrupted us to say: "Miles, you've got your first table of the night. It's a group of two."

I found a place to put my gift, collected myself and got to work. After filling two glasses with water and placing them on a tray, I approached a table with a couple of elderly women sitting at it. We exchanged a warm hello, and then I introduced myself and asked the bright, jovial women if they were celebrating anything in particular that night. They smiled, looked at each other, and announced that they were both celebrating their eighty-fifth birthdays that week.

"That's amazing," I replied, wishing them each a happy birthday before taking a drink order.

A different kind of power

Over the next few hours, those birthday girls slowly ordered salads, appetizers, and main courses as the restaurant filled with a bustling Friday night crowd. By the time they were finished eating, I was busily running around the restaurant, but I made sure to take the time to offer them each a free birthday dessert. They were both happy to accept this gift.

I brought them two slices of cheesecake with little candles on top. Those grandmothers' eyes lit up like young girls as I placed their special birthday treats in front of them.

After finishing every last bite of their desserts, my birthday guests asked for their bill. And a few minutes later, when I finished taking their payment, I decided it was the perfect moment to ask them a question I'd been waiting to pose all night.

"Okay, ladies," I said, "you're both celebrating eighty-five years of life on Earth. Given everything you've seen and experienced, what's the most important advice you can share? What wisdom do you have for a guy like me?"

The women smiled, and without hesitating, one answered: "Be very careful who you choose to be with in this life. It's the most important decision you will ever make."

She spoke with a gravity that caught me off guard, staring into my eyes to make sure I understood the seriousness of her words. Her companion sat across the table, nodding in agreement, then added: "You seem like a nice guy - you could get eaten alive if you chose the wrong person."

Seven

For the next five minutes, I stood between those elders as they told me how both of their daughters married men who betrayed and used them in various ways.

"I could see it coming from the start," one of the women said, "but my daughter wouldn't listen. She was blinded by his charms - blinded by her feelings and what she wanted to believe."

The other woman nodded in agreement, sharing how the same thing happened to her daughter - and all she could do was stand back and watch, knowing exactly what was going to occur.

"When your family and friends try to warn you that you've chosen the wrong one," she explained, "you need to listen. And trust your gut, too. I don't want to see a news story about how someone took advantage of or destroyed you. And if I do, I'll be able to say that I told you so. I'll look and tell everyone: *'Hey, I warned that guy!'* I've done my job - you've been warned."

We all laughed, and I thanked them for this unusual, grave advice before wishing them a happy birthday one more time and saying goodbye. As I walked away from them, the words "you've been warned" haunted me. Something about that moment with those grandmothers felt surreal. I had stood before them in awe - their answer to my innocent question carrying a kind of weight and specificity I hadn't been prepared for. They seemed to have had their response prepared - immediately and unanimously delivering their stern, solemn warning to the naive young man before them when he asked his question. It also struck me that they had no way of knowing if I was single. They never asked me about that. But, maybe, being the wise elders they were, they could smell it on me. Perhaps they could smell my naivety and vulnerability. Maybe they saw a weakness of mine just as clearly as they had seen it in their daughters.

As I stumbled to the back of the restaurant, I felt like I could explode with excitement. I picked up the book Angel had just given me and reread the subtitle: *"One choice can destroy you."*

For the next hour, I walked around the restaurant, laughing like I was in on a joke with the universe that nobody else could see or understand. When my coworker, Sara, noticed this and asked what I was so happy about, I told her it was nothing.

"Something's going on," she replied, too perceptive and curious to let it be.

After a moment of hesitation, I explained what had just happened. I told Sara about the inner conflict I'd been wrestling with when I got to work that afternoon. I shared my strong gut sense that this was a time to remain patient and not rush into any impulsive romance - that doing so could have far-reaching consequences at this fertile moment. Then, I showed her the book Angel had given me and watched as her eyes widened at the ominous subtitle. I described the stark warning those grandmothers had delivered and my astonishment at it all.

With a look of disbelief, Sara stared into my eyes and said: "You're being protected, Miles."

Seven

We suddenly remembered the many people waiting for us at tables throughout the restaurant, and the chaos of the evening forced us to scatter in separate directions.

Over the following days, I thought a lot about the words of those grandmothers. I'd asked many people the same question I posed to them over the years - usually elderly folks who felt particularly vital and bright - but I had never gotten that answer. Usually, the words of wisdom I received centred around being grateful, staying active, and appreciating the little things. Those were profound answers. And, as I reflected on the unique response of those elderly women, I realized something: It's a lot easier to be grateful and appreciate the little things when you have good people around. It's much easier to be happy when your life is peaceful. One negative, destructive, or dramatic relationship can make that kind of gracious perspective desperately challenging to maintain. Negativity is powerfully contagious. Given this, maybe their answer was complementary to the more common responses - a fundamental piece of what makes a positive, empowered way of living life possible.

I did not begin to read the book Angel gave me after I brought it home. But it found a place on my bookshelf and lived there more as a symbol and a reminder than anything else. It was a beautiful gift, and when I looked at it, I thought of my kind, inspired coworker - as well as those grannies and their unforgettable words of warning and wisdom. More than anything, the book reminded me of something easy to say but challenging to do: *Listen to your gut.* And now, if I chose not to listen, I couldn't say I hadn't been warned.

Eight

Near the end of a long and busy night at the restaurant, I noticed a woman sitting at a table by herself. All the other servers had finished and gone home for the evening, so I was left alone to handle any remaining tables and was rushing from one end of the restaurant to another, trying my best to keep up with everyone I was serving.

When I had a moment, I approached this solitary guest, introduced myself, and asked her if there was anything that she would like right away. Her presence was instantly warm, kind, and gentle. This was a welcome reprieve after an evening of interactions with several rude and impatient guests. We spoke for a few minutes, and I explained some menu items to her before disappearing to tend to my other tables.

When I eventually returned, she ordered a small meal and a large glass of red wine. She mentioned she'd been struggling with some kind of health issue and that this was the first time she'd eaten out at a restaurant in years. So, I recognized that this was a special occasion.

A different kind of power

After hearing that piece of information, I stood up a bit straighter and treated her with greater care and intention. The more we spoke, the more I could feel what a sweet soul this woman had.

After rushing away to tend to another customer, I got caught up taking payments and chatting with people. After ten or fifteen minutes passed, I realized I'd forgotten to check in on my solitary guest and marched back to her table, embarrassed. When I arrived, she seemed completely unbothered and happy, sharing that this was one of the most beautiful evenings she'd had in ages. The food was phenomenal, she said - but she explained that she couldn't eat much. Her health was still recovering from a series of illnesses and setbacks - and because of that, she didn't have much of an appetite. The wine, she told me, was the best part. She didn't usually drink wine. But this, according to her, was a special night. It had been a long time since she had treated herself like this.

With all my other guests now finished and gone, I had time to linger and speak with this warm, gentle woman, who seemed more than happy to talk. As we chatted, she told me about some of her health challenges, her daughters, and her many beloved pets - whose healing energy kept her filled with love and life, she said.

At one point in our conversation, she briefly mentioned her childhood experience being put into an Indigenous residential school and how devastating it had been. In Canada, residential schools were government-run institutions where Indigenous children

Eight

- who were forcibly removed from their families and communities - were abused, indoctrinated, and treated in ways that no child anywhere should ever be treated.

As this beautiful woman spoke for a moment about being an innocent child faced with such a heartbreaking nightmare, I felt the power of her words, and my eyes filled with tears.

"I'm so sorry that happened to you," I said. "No one should ever be put through what you went through."

On the verge of bawling my eyes out, I took a deep breath and clung to the tiny, vanishing thread of strength I had left to contain myself and keep my composure as she spoke.

Then, as though nothing had happened, my gracious guest shifted gears - changing the subject and cracking a joke about a silly friend of hers. Instead of laughing with her, however, I strained to hold back tears and stood across from her in awkward silence. She looked at me confused, as though the friendly guy she'd been laughing and getting along with all night had suddenly gotten weird and lost his sense of humour. Before this disconnect could grow more uncomfortable, I excused myself and said I'd return shortly.

As I walked to the back of the dark, empty restaurant, I decided I needed to do something for this gentle woman. I realized I should pay for her meal. Given what she'd just shared with me, it was the least I could do to show that I saw her, appreciated her, and was heartbroken by what she'd been put through as a kid. More than anything, I was in awe of the kind and beautiful spirit she possessed.

A different kind of power

With the wheels in my head turning, my manager, Brock, walked past me and asked: "Everything okay, Miles?"

Without thinking, I answered: "Yeah. There's this woman I'm serving, and she's a residential school survivor. We just talked about life and what she's been through for ten minutes. And I feel like I need to do something for her."

"You want us to take care of the bill?" he asked straightforwardly.

Before I could think, I replied: "Ummm - yeah."

"Okay," Brock said. "Thanks for saying something - this is the right thing to do. You can go ahead and tell her that we wanted to do something nice for her tonight, and dinner's on us."

Surprised that Brock had walked by at that moment and done for me what I'd been planning on doing with my own money, I thanked him sincerely before heading back to my lone guest.

"Oh, there you are," she said warmly as I approached. "I'm ready for the bill anytime, hun. You've been such a sweetheart!"

I smiled, took a breath, and said: "There's no bill for you tonight. We took care of it."

She stared up at me with a look of confusion before replying: "What?"

Suddenly unsure of myself and how this gesture was going to be received, I knelt down beside her and explained: "You shared something that really moved me tonight when we were talking, and I just wanted to

Eight

show my appreciation for that - I wanted to show my appreciation for you."

"What do you mean!?" she asked, still perplexed by what exactly I was trying to say.

"We took care of your bill tonight. It's on us. You inspired me with your story and your kindness, and I just wanted to do something - however small - to say thank you for that."

Suddenly, she burst into tears. "Why are you being so nice to me?" she asked, shouting through heavy sobs. "Are you an angel?!"

I laughed and replied: "No, I think I'm just doing what is obvious. You shared something that moved me, and I wanted to honour that."

As I spoke, her crying intensified. I wondered if I'd done something wrong - if somehow this gesture had been an error in judgment and unintentionally opened something vulnerable and raw. But, rather than flinching or reacting, I realized that it was her turn to feel the tears, and my job was to breathe and be there with her. Tears filled my eyes, too - but I didn't break my composure or weep. It wasn't my time to fall apart.

Still crying, my guest shared: "Everything about this night was supposed to happen. As soon as I sat down at this table, I said to myself: *I feel like I've been here before. This is all so familiar.* It was deja vu. And I felt it all night!" She paused briefly, still sobbing, before continuing: "I was supposed to meet you here tonight. This was all meant to happen - I knew something was up!"

A different kind of power

Her words sent chills down my spine, and I nodded. For the next ten minutes, we spoke through tears about the meaning of that moment, our ancestors watching over us, her daughters, her pets, and so much more. For that moment, we weren't strangers in a fancy restaurant - we were two souls connected in a way that language can barely describe. Time seemed to stop, and we were both unfiltered in our words of praise and appreciation - though I did quite a bit more listening than speaking.

Eventually, I remembered we were still in a restaurant and excused myself so this lovely woman could finish her glass of wine in peace. We exchanged a warm hug and shared more words of gratitude before I disappeared.

A few minutes later, I was cleaning up in the back when one of the teenage bussers approached me and said: "Hey, Miles, there's someone at the front of the restaurant asking for you."

Smiling, I realized that my special guest was probably ready to leave for the night, and I made my way to see her. When I got to the front of the restaurant, I saw a woman who looked completely different from the person I'd been speaking to and crying with minutes earlier. I knew it was her, but something had profoundly changed. She had put on a stylish jacket and hat, but the difference I saw wasn't superficial. A brilliant smile was stretched across her face, and a light shined in her eyes - she was absolutely glowing.

"There's my friend!" she said with exuberance. "Miles, you are a beautiful soul. Thank you so much for tonight. I will see you again. I know it."

Eight

We exchanged a couple more hugs as we shared parting words of praise and gratitude, and I felt the significance of something she said as she repeated it: *I will see you again.*

The way she said those words, or how I received them, made it feel like we were meant to cross paths in this lifetime - and somehow, we would do so again.

I thanked her for sharing some of her kindness and grace with me and told her she was an inspiration. Then we said one last goodbye before she turned around and walked proudly out of that restaurant - a radiant, powerful woman.

As I returned to the back of the building by myself and continued my end-of-night chores - spraying down and wiping countertops, emptying garbage bins, etc - I found myself reeling from what had just happened. Something about that interaction felt more powerful than I could comprehend. As I hauled a full garbage bag down to the dumpster, I was convinced that everything in my life had been preparing me for that moment. Everything I had gone through - every mistake I made that burned a painful lesson into me, every loss or experience that helped me grow - all of my life had been for this: To be able to notice that stranger, ask them about themselves, then shut up and listen. To be able to see their beauty and do something to acknowledge it.

On the surface, what we'd done for her was a very simple gesture. We gave her a couple glasses of wine and a bite to eat. I knew it wasn't a significant act at all. But what it led to was profound. She was a woman who had been through things I couldn't fathom - yet,

A different kind of power

somehow, seemed more kind and gentle than most all others. She held a strange and phenomenal light - a different kind of power than I commonly encountered. And I was blessed to have come into contact with it.

In the weeks and months that followed that experience, I carried the memory of it like a gift - holding it as a source of light and warmth when I found myself conflicted by moments of fear, self-doubt, or drama. When the reality of being a deeply flawed human felt like too heavy a weight on my shoulders, I would remember that night in the restaurant. And strangely, something about it helped everything feel more bearable. I was human, and I made mistakes. But that one time, the same sensitivity and inner fire that could get me into trouble pushed me to make a stranger into a friend - even if it was just for a passing moment.

Something sacred was exchanged in that fleeting interaction - some special wisdom, power, or love that woman shared with me - and I knew I would never forget it. And who knows, maybe she was right, and I will see her again one day.

Nine

My parents were passing through town for an afternoon in late winter when we met up for a visit. I greeted them near my apartment building, where they found some convenient parking, and invited them to see my humble little home for the first time. They had brought me some gifts: Homemade dill pickles and some of my Dad's smoked sockeye salmon. Returning to my place for a moment allowed me to drop off these special presents.

After arriving at my building and climbing the stairs to my floor, we entered my tiny studio apartment, and I announced: "Well, this is it. I can give you the full tour without any of us moving or even turning our heads."

They stared with quiet curiosity at the desk where I worked and entertained myself, the futon where I sat while writing multiple books, the mini fridge and kitchen counter (with a small hot plate on it for cooking), and the handful of houseplants I shared my space with. With some embarrassment, I acknowledged that this home wasn't really big enough to be fully functional, but before I could finish what I was saying, my Father cut me off.

"You're happy here, though," he said. "You've got everything you need, and it's nice. This is perfect for you!"

I thought for a second before responding: "You're right. It's true - I'm happy. And, to be honest, this is only part of my home. The other part is the forest I live beside. That's really my backyard - I spend so much time there, it feels like an extension of my living space."

After completing a quick home tour and dropping off the gifts my parents had brought, we left my building and decided to go for a walk around the neighbourhood. Given that we were moments away from the forested park I'd just been speaking about, we decided that would be the perfect place for a stroll.

As we walked out of my building and onto the quiet street beside it, my Mother stopped to look at something in the distance for a moment before exclaiming: "Wow, this is incredible, Miles. You actually spent some time right here as a young child."

Curious to know more, I asked my Mother what she was talking about. She replied: "When you were about three years old, we had a big house fire and had to move out of our place while repairs were being done."

I had no conscious memory of this house fire, but I'd heard about it countless times over the years - a freak accident caused by a Lego set placed on a stovetop and some of my Father's friends having a bit too much fun. Nobody was hurt during the fire, but I knew we had to

Nine

leave our home afterwards because the damage it caused was so extensive.

My Mother continued: "Well, this is where we came to stay during that time." She pointed to a building just around the corner from my apartment. "For a few months, this was where we lived. And it was beautiful. I'd take you and your brothers for walks in the park here every day. And you were all so young at the time - you kids were in heaven. With all the ducks, raccoons, and squirrels to watch, you boys loved it. It really was the perfect place to be able to go with you. I loved that time here so much."

We walked up to the building where I'd apparently lived all those years ago - just across the street and around the corner from my apartment.

"It's pretty wild that you ended up here again," my Mother remarked. "What are the odds that you arrived right back at this place decades later? It's almost spooky, really."

I agreed, quietly taking this information in as I looked at the old building. We carried on our way, entering the park and walking an easy, short route around the water as we chatted about life. At one point, my Mother commented: "I remember taking you guys right here. You loved it so much - you were in heaven."

"I bet," I replied. "This place is like a natural zoo - there's such an abundance of vibrant plant and animal life, it would be a child's dream come true."

After a brief walk in the park, we made our way toward a busy main street with plenty of restaurants, and my Dad chose one for us to have dinner at together.

A different kind of power

When we finished there, I walked my parents back to their car, hugged them, told them I loved them, and said goodbye. It was a brief visit, as they were quickly travelling through the city before catching a flight. But I was grateful to see them - and to give them a glimpse of my simple life.

Over the following days, something about my Mother's revelation that I had lived in this neighbourhood before haunted me. It struck me that when I first moved into my apartment, I hadn't been talking to my parents for years. There was no way I could have consciously known that I lived at this very place on Earth before. And I couldn't help but wonder if somehow, for some reason, I had been pulled back to it.

On my morning walks in the forest, I recalled my Mother's words: *I remember taking you guys right here. You loved it so much - you were in heaven.* Now, as a grown man, I took myself to this place every day - and I was in heaven.

This forest may have been one of the first places where I ever felt the magic of the natural world as a child. And I wondered if my heart had formed some kind of special bond with the beauty of this sacred place - this sanctuary of trees and pure life energy in the city. After hearing my Mother recount the basic facts, it was hard for me to look at it any other way.

Five years earlier, when I moved into this neighbourhood, my life was at a particularly low point - the lowest it had ever been. I was alone and confused - slowly coming to terms with the cold reality of a life

Nine

that looked and felt nothing like what I'd hoped, imagined, or expected it to be.

My world didn't get much brighter for the first couple of years there. I fell in love briefly, but that was gone as quickly as it came. And, in the wake of that loss, I was left alone again - a bit more confused than before, with a fresh feeling of emptiness in my life.

Then, with the pain of a newly broken heart aching in me, something extraordinary happened: I went outside. I went for a long, meandering walk in the forest I lived at the edge of, and when I stumbled home afterwards, I felt better. I felt so much better - and was so desperate for some kind of relief - that I began walking in that forest every morning. This ritual of spending time outdoors and among the trees lifted my spirit in such a significant way - filling my world with something so precious and vital - that I quickly decided it was a necessity. I almost never missed a day.

Over several years, these walks - and my relationship with that forest - took on a depth and significance that I could not have predicted. What began as a convenient, healthy way of enjoying exercise and reflection in a beautiful, natural setting slowly evolved into a life-changing, intimate connection. In the silent peace of those woods, I spent countless hours digesting life experiences - talking things out that had been weighing heavy on my mind and heart as they revealed themselves in the emptiness of that space. With the trees, squirrels, and ferns as my witnesses, I had conversations with myself, with life, with lost friends, and with nothing in particular. I raged, laughed, cried, and stared in awe at the majesty of the life that surrounded me as it constantly changed. And, ever so slowly, a magic that I had almost completely lost - a pure, innocent, and sacred inner power - began to flicker back into my awareness.

There were many moments during these years when I wondered if I was stuck in a rut and needed to take dramatic actions to shake up my monotonous life. I'd been living for what seemed like far too long in a tiny little apartment, working the same dead-end job, and chronically single. But whenever I began to question the possible stagnation of my life, I remembered the forest. In my gut, I felt like I'd been put in the perfect place, at the edge of two worlds, to be healed by that forest. And I knew I wasn't done yet. Not even close.

To learn that I'd been here before and met this place as a child - with an innocent heart completely open to its beauty - was astonishing and made perfect sense. Maybe, when I needed it most, that child pulled me back here - knowing there was a power in the forest that could help me. Or, maybe it was the forest itself calling that kid home. Either way, I got there, and I knew I was blessed. So, when I fell into the trap of comparing myself to others and wondering what was wrong with me for being so weird or boring, I remembered the forest. And when I didn't have the strength to remember it, I did at least have the sense to go there.

Nine

One morning, while walking in the forest, I got the urge to touch a massive, old-growth Douglas fir tree at the side of the trail I was on. I stopped, looked both ways and hesitated - I couldn't face the embarrassment of being seen by a stranger while touching or hugging a tree. But the urge to connect with a tree physically felt too strong and pure to ignore completely. So, I decided to make my way to a quiet spot off the beaten path, where I could express myself more freely without the fear of being seen. As I turned to walk toward a secluded, private spot, I stopped and asked myself: *Why are you still hiding?*

I looked back at the massive old fir tree I felt so drawn to. As I stood and stared at the broad trunk of that ancient, towering life form, the question in my mind began to feel more like a provocation: *What are you ashamed of? When will you finally be proud of embracing beauty?*

I looked both ways again to see if anyone was coming down the trail. Nobody was there, but I knew it shouldn't make any difference either way. In my heart, I felt that bowing down at the base of that tree and touching its trunk in reverence might be one of the most beautiful things I ever do - not something to be ashamed of or embarrassed by. And I got the overwhelming sense in that moment that this mattered - that listening to the voice telling me to touch that tree really mattered. So I took a deep breath, walked up to that stunning ancient tree, placed my hands on its rough, deeply furrowed bark, and closed my eyes.

A different kind of power

I let myself simply be there for a few moments - though not without self-conscious apprehensions. I was challenging myself to do something weird and unusual in public without caring what others thought. As I stood with my eyes closed, I heard a cyclist cruise by on the coarse trail behind me and felt my insides squirm as I maintained contact with the tree. Strangers slowly walked past, and at moments, I felt like jumping out of my body, I was so self-conscious.

But seconds later, when I dropped into the moment completely and let myself soak up the sanctity of it, I felt incredible. As my hands clung to that tree's furrowed bark, I felt the strength and stability of this silent, centuries-old sentinel of the forest move through my palms and into me, calming the frantic activity of my anxious mind and body. Being starved as I was for any kind of physical touch, the mere act of holding that tree trunk felt like medicine, and for a minute, I let myself luxuriate in it. As I took deep breaths, my mind slowed down, and I dropped the normal barriers to connection and intimacy that I moved through the world with, opening my heart to the beautiful energy of the tree. After a short burst of uninhibited connection, I sent feelings of love to this spectacular being, looked up at its trunk reaching far into the sky, and removed my hands from it. Stumbling backwards onto the trail, I said a quiet thank you before continuing my walk, grateful that I'd found the courage to touch something so beautiful.

The next morning, I took the same route on my walk and returned to that fir tree. Again, I stared at its

Nine

towering body, in awe of its massive, almost supernatural form. I approached its trunk with reverence, and before I could hesitate or entertain my fears, placed my hands on two perfectly shaped burls of bark, closed my eyes, and let myself feel. Standing in silence, I felt the enormity and power of that tree - a power that was quiet, stable, and patient. My mind slowed down to the pace of this giant elder, and I felt the silent wisdom of its mere existence move through me.

Then, I heard the rhythmic footsteps of a jogger bounding along the forest path, quickly approaching. I fought the urge to stop what I was doing and act normal, reminding myself that I was no longer going to hide things I felt were wholesome and beautiful. So, while my ego squirmed, I remained exactly where I was - eyes closed, hands against the tree.

The jogger quickly passed, and I realized that this meditation was now just as much about connecting with the tree as it was about becoming comfortable in my own skin. With my hands still pressed against the fir tree's bark, I let my thoughts go quiet and enjoyed the moment.

After those first two mornings at the fir tree, I made visiting it a daily ritual. There was something sacred about this - a moment of quiet, physical connection with a living thing that contrasted all else in my world. It seemed like a natural evolution of the walks I'd been going on for years - bringing a new dimension of depth and intimacy that I didn't want to go without for even one day. When I arrived at the base of that behemoth of

A different kind of power

a tree, I would look up at its body reaching into the sky, then down to the Earth, where its trunk sprawled out and descended beneath the forest floor, spreading into a network of massive, powerful roots that supported it. Once I'd soaked in the enormity of its presence, I would place my hands on it, close my eyes, and just be there. People walked, jogged, and biked past, and though my embarrassment and urge to hide slowly diminished, it was still in me. So, every morning, while I kept my hands on that tree, I reminded myself that this was not something to be ashamed of.

One such morning, I was holding the tree when a family slowly walked past. I heard their footsteps and snippets of quiet conversation as I stayed still. I felt the tree's energy wrap around me like a protector, surrounding me with its power and emboldening me to stand strong regardless of how I was seen.

The family slowly moved along. When I felt complete with my moment of connection, I opened my eyes, dropped my hands, and stepped back toward the trail. I then realized that the family was still standing mere feet away. One of them - the oldest man of the group - smiled at me before asking: "Did you feel its energy?"

A bit stoned and blissed out from what I'd just been doing, I reflected for a moment before responding: "I did. It's really big."

The man grinned and looked at me with a sparkle in his eyes - as though he knew exactly what I was talking about. He said nothing, quietly nodding his head before turning and walking down the trail with his family. I

Nine

looked back at the sacred tree towering above me, then smiled and thought: *Maybe I'm not so weird after all.* Given the look in that man's eyes and the sincerity of his words, I got the impression that to him, this was the farthest thing from weird. On the contrary, it seemed that he saw something pure and sacred which touched a place deeper than language could express. With a feeling of joy in my heart, I thanked the beautiful tree and made my way onward.

A few days later, I was back at the fir tree - my hands on its deeply crevassed bark, eyes closed, and my forehead pressed against its trunk. For several minutes, I let my love and admiration for the tree flow out of me and meditated on its power and beauty. Its age, size, and stillness seemed to put me and my world into perspective. I was told it had been living in that place for over five centuries - long before the entire city surrounding it existed. It had stood there in silence for hundreds of years, towering above the people as countless human lifetimes came and went. It survived wildfires and colonial deforestation by some miraculous strokes of luck. Souls walked past it during many eras, some of whom were likely consumed by worries, fears, dreams, and desires that must have seemed fleeting from a larger, centuries-wide perspective.

Standing there, leaning my head against its base, I felt how ant-like, fast-paced, and emotionally reactive my very nature as a human was in comparison to this stoic, unflinching monument of power. It made me laugh, and it was a beautiful contrast to witness. With more and more of my time being spent in front of a

A different kind of power

screen of some kind, interacting with a landscape of technology and creation that seemed purposefully designed to fuel the small-minded, neurotic, and self-absorbed aspects of my being, this communion with a different kind of power felt like a much-needed tonic.

After several minutes, I opened my eyes, looked up at my tree-friend, and said thank you. As I walked down a trail and made my way onward, my heart was filled with a glowing, melting sensation. I wasn't sure if I'd ever felt quite this good before.

Bursting with love and gratitude, I smiled and offered warm hellos to every stranger I walked past, noticing that a few of them seemed to be staring at me rather intently. A couple of beautiful young women, in particular, had their eyes fixed on my face. *It must be the energy,* I thought to myself, bouncing along the trail with a renewed sense of faith in life.

When I got back to my apartment, I headed to the washroom, where I caught a glimpse of myself in the mirror and noticed something out of place: There was a large chunk of brown stuff on my forehead, directly where I'd been leaning it against the bark of that special tree. My eyes widened, and I realized that it looked like I had a big piece of poo on my face. The curious looks of the strangers I had just been smiling at and saying hello to (including those beautiful young women) suddenly made sense. I removed the large, suspicious-looking chunk of bark from my forehead, laughing so hard I almost cried. Given everything, I couldn't possibly bother with feeling embarrassed by this. Even if everyone I just said hello to thought I had been walking

Nine

around with a piece of feces on my face, considering what I was feeling, it was worth it. Maybe some of the perspective and wisdom of that ancient tree had gotten into me - because, at that moment, the trivial judgements and superficial opinions of strangers meant about as much as the concerns of an earthworm or an ant. I'd just touched something so big that if I made a fool of myself on the tail end of that, it didn't matter. For that moment, I was pretty sure I'd been given a taste of pure enlightenment.

During one of my routine visits to the big old fir tree, I again placed my hands on its trunk, closed my eyes, and let myself feel the enormity of the divine being I was with. For several minutes, I drifted into a meditation, my imagination filling the empty space with visualizations of herculean tree roots spreading down and out through the forest floor beneath me. As I drifted into this, I heard what I can only describe as the tree's voice whisper in my mind: *"You're one of us, now."*

Given my slightly altered state of consciousness, this message was less surprising than I would have expected. So, more curious than alarmed, I stayed where I was and wondered what that statement meant.

Then, the tree repeated itself: *"You're one of us now."* And this time, I knew exactly what it meant. Somehow, I could feel within those words that, as far as the tree was concerned, I had become one of *them* - one of the patient, strong beings who wasn't afraid of standing firm in their truth, even if the whole world didn't understand. As I rested there, eyes closed, face pressed into the trunk of that tree, I realized I had stopped caring about being seen doing this quite some time ago. My morning ritual had become a practice in doing what the tree did so magnificently: Being myself and staying rooted in that.

I remained where I was, and the phrase, *"You're one of us now,"* slowly repeated. Tears filled my eyes. So much was communicated beneath those words - an acceptance, love, and solidarity as firm as the Earth I was standing on. It was almost intimidating - a centuries-old giant suggesting that I was one of *them*. My pettiness and fragility seemed so deeply entrenched that I wasn't sure if this was a designation I could possibly live up to. Eventually, I let go of the tree, stepped away, and thanked it before continuing my walk - my heart filled with a sense of strength and belonging.

I knew this was a next level to my fascination with the forest: Now, I was talking to and hearing back from trees. To an outsider, it might appear that I was indulging in some wild delusions or suffering from an overactive imagination. But I figured that even if this was purely my imagination or delusion, it was still probably the healthiest thing I had going for me.

On one of my walks during this time, I took an alternate route to the fir tree. I noticed a group of enormous old-growth cedars along the way. I'd marvelled at these trees many times over the years, but

Nine

this morning, I felt compelled to connect with one of them in particular. It was a massive western red cedar with an unfathomably wide trunk that supported three large pillars that split off from its base in mid-air and reached up to the sky. By now, I had discovered that if I paid attention, every tree, like every person, had a distinct energy. On a couple occasions, I'd felt curious to touch an unfamiliar tree and immediately felt something that just wasn't right - as though we weren't a good match for each other and our chemistry was off. As I stared at this remarkable cedar, I suspected we might have good chemistry. Without hesitating, I approached, found the perfect spot to stand at its base, and placed my hands on its smooth bark.

I instantly felt a wave of relaxation wash over me. The soft, longitudinal striations of this tree's bark were a stark contrast to the hard, rough, and bumpy surface of the Douglas fir I had become so familiar with. As my bare hands registered this palpable difference, my body was filled with a gentle, nurturing, almost maternal energy that perfectly complemented the tactile sensation of its bark. My eyes closed, and I let myself fill up with this exquisite feeling. People occasionally walked past as I stood there, and I didn't budge. There was something too special happening to care what they might think.

After connecting to that big old fir tree for so long, it was incredible to notice how different this cedar's energy was. In a way, the fir tree felt like a father - hard, stoic, protective, and steadfast. And this cedar felt like a mother - soft, loving, nurturing, and benevolent. I felt

A different kind of power

myself melting into its soft, feminine energy - my own stoic, solitary spirit being nourished and balanced by something so beautifully different from me.

As I continued to lean against it, I suddenly decided that this cedar was a *mother* tree, and the ancient fir I'd been getting to know over the previous months was a *father*. That was exactly how they both felt.

After some time, I heard what I can only describe as the voice of this cedar quietly whispering something to me in the back of my mind. It said it had heard about me - that the fir tree I'd been visiting daily had told it all about me. According to this cedar, the fir tree thought very highly of me - as though I was an exciting new friend it couldn't help but brag to everyone about.

My hands were still fixed on the cedar's smooth, soft bark, and this all somehow made perfect sense. Perhaps the trees communicated underground through vast networks of roots and mycelium. It didn't really matter how. At that moment, it just made sense that these trees would know each other. They were some of the oldest residents of that forest, after all. They had both been growing there since long before the city of Vancouver existed. They might have both been growing there since well before the first European colonists set foot anywhere near that part of the continent. Given this, they probably knew some things.

After some time, I felt a sense of completion and let go of the trunk of that cedar before stepping back from it and saying, "Thank you."

A few minutes later, when I arrived for my daily pilgrimage to the old fir tree, I swear I could feel its

Nine

excitement to see me. And when I placed my hands on its burly trunk, there was a sense of joy at two friends being together again. I also noticed that where the mother tree had felt so soft and nurturing, this father tree did indeed feel hard, strong, and steady. More than anything, it amazed me how much it felt as though that fir tree liked me. As I stood there and showered it with love and affection, I felt its energy wrap around me as though it was giving me a hug. And, when the time felt right, I stepped away and said thank you, once again filled with wonder and gratitude.

After that first visit to the mother tree, I began to go back every day. It wasn't something I understood, but I felt like I had another friend now, and it only made sense to visit and connect with that friend daily. As time passed, I marvelled at how every day with these trees was different. There were days when I felt held, protected, and nurtured by them. There were days when I simply showered them with love and gratitude, letting it pour out from my heart through my hands and into their trunks. The more time I spent with these giants, the more my feelings of connection with each of them evolved - not unlike a close human relationship. And, perhaps because I was so completely uninhibited and emotionally open in their presence, I could feel the shifts in our dynamic deeply as they happened. As months passed, I forgot about the monikers of the mother and father tree. Those labels didn't make sense or fit anymore - the trees were just themselves. I needed to continually throw away any preconceptions or expectations I formed about these beings as I got to

A different kind of power

know them better. Rather than approaching them with assumptions about how or who they might be based on previous experiences, I went with an open mind to admire, listen, learn, and pay my respects - never clinging too tightly to what I thought I knew about them.

There were days when I visited them, placed my hands on their trunks, and felt nothing. I was too filled with internal noise from the dramas and worries of life. And there were days when I simply felt a quiet sense of peace and admiration for their beauty. Over time, that became the most common experience.

When I felt compelled to give one of them a full-on hug, I had to force myself, once again, to shelve my self-consciousness and risk being judged for the sake of something sacred. And when I took my shoes off to feel the soft forest floor beneath my feet while with them, I completed my look as an unhinged hippie and enhanced my sense of connection to the Earth.

One afternoon, I was on my way home after running some errands - feeling more down and depressed than usual for reasons I did not understand. As thoughts of disillusionment with myself for things I hadn't achieved or experienced consumed me, I saw an acquaintance, Paul, walking on the opposite side of the street. The last time I saw Paul, he had been in an uncharacteristically depressed state. Typically an upbeat, driven, and

Nine

focused man, we'd spoken for quite a while about what he described as a sudden, total loss of motivation - a sense of being utterly disinterested in life without any purpose, direction, or inspiration.

Paul, like me, was a writer. He recently completed a book he'd been working on passionately. And as soon as that project was done, he lost his motivation to do anything. Previously, he'd always jumped from one project or enterprise to another - constantly engaged with some kind of challenge or endeavour. But now, for the first time in his life, there was nothing. He had no drive to do anything whatsoever - and it horrified him. The spark he'd had throughout all of his life was gone, and he was adrift.

After listening to Paul explain his situation, I offered another perspective (which I believe was influenced by the ancient trees I'd been holding minutes earlier): "None of that sounds unusual or bad, Paul. For most of us, inspiration and creativity come in seasons. And sometimes, there are seasons where you just need to drink in the beauty of life. There's nothing else to do. It might be a time to just live and collect new experiences. It might just be time to drink in the beauty of life."

When we said goodbye at the end of that conversation, Paul announced: "Okay, I'm going to go and try to do that right now. I will go into the forest and try to do that - drink in life."

Nearly a month had passed since that meeting, so when I saw Paul in the distance on this particular afternoon, I was excited to hear how he had been doing. When he noticed me, Paul quickly marched across the street. And when he got near, he stared into my eyes with a menacing gaze and said: "Drink in the beauty of life! Miles, you were right - just drink in the beauty of life! That's what I've been doing since we last talked - and it's everything."

Paul's eyes glowed intensely as though he was high on a phenomenal drug, and I quickly realized that he was. He'd been drinking in the beauty of life.

"That was exactly what I needed to hear when I last saw you, Miles," he continued. "Thank you so much - those were the perfect words!"

I laughed and expressed my happiness that Paul had found his spark again. Then, without any further ado, he thanked me once more before marching on with a bounce in his step.

As I watched him walk away, beaming, I thought to myself: "Damn, Paul is *really* drinking it in."

Then, I realized the profundity of his words: *Drink in the beauty of life, Miles.*

At that moment, I could not have received a more perfect message. I'd run into Paul at a moment of deflation and listlessness, and I suppose it was his turn to hold the torch:

Just drink in the beauty of life.

Paul was so filled up with that beauty that it was contagious, and I stumbled home from our brief exchange with a kind of contact high. It was a beautiful gift to receive, instantly pulling me out of my funk and grounding me into the precious reality of that moment.

What made it even more interesting was that those words had come through me a month earlier after I

Nine

stumbled out of the forest with a natural high - and then returned when I needed to hear them. Maybe that's how kindness or love works: You give it when you have it to give. And you give it from your heart, even when it's scary. Because when the time comes that you need it, it will be out there, alive in others, moving through the world, and it might even reach back to you.

From the author

To anyone who has taken the time to read this far, thank you for welcoming this book and these stories into your world. I hope you have enjoyed them, and if you have, there are several ways you can easily help the book and its message spread. Leaving a rating or review on Amazon and other online marketplaces helps tremendously and enables others to find and connect with it. I also always feel immensely grateful for such feedback.

If you're curious to know what I'm up to and would like to stay updated about future books etc, visit *milesolsen.com*, where you can join my mailing list and see what I'm working on.

Again, thank you so much for reading.

Made in United States
North Haven, CT
03 November 2024